THE SONOMA POLICE REPORT
FUNNY, ODD TALES
FROM THE WINE COUNTRY

JOSHUA FARRELL

The Sonoma Police Report: funny, odd tales from the wine country

Published in the United States by Schellville, Inc.
ISBN 978-0-9899345-0-3

Cover Concept: Joshua Farrell
Cover Design: Kirsten Farrell
Interior Design: Amy Segal-Burke

For my Mom and Dad, who raised me in Sonoma,
laughed a lot, and almost kept me out
of the Police Report.

Contents

Sonoma is the most beautiful, idyllic, and romantic place. Always relaxing, wine in hand, taking strolls through vineyards. It doesn't get any better than that.

-Eileen, Sonoma Tourist

Sonoma was like Mayberry on Acid.

- Ken, Sonoma Mayor

INTRODUCTION

When people ask me where I was raised and I tell them, "Sonoma," it's usually followed with a lot of Ooo's and Ahhs and comments such as, "You're soooo lucky!" "Did you grow up in a vineyard?" "It's like growing up in a storybook, isn't it?" I feel quite lucky and very grateful for being raised in Sonoma for reasons very different than people would think. No, I didn't grow up in a vineyard, and my parents didn't own a winery. We had a lumberyard.

What I love about Sonoma has nothing to do with vineyards, its romantic views, or its "top 10" guidebook rating. I love Sonoma because of the Sonomans. I grew up with and continue to meet some of the funniest, kookiest, most interesting, and creative people I've ever met anywhere. People who like to work hard, party, cook, create art, play music, mentor kids, go to baseball games, etc. Friends made in childhood stay friends for life.

I got the idea for this book because I've always loved this town and have been fascinated with it's eccentricities. And that can be most evident in the police reports. When I was a kid, I wanted to be a police officer. I used to volunteer to help out at the old station on Patten Street. I also used to read the police report religiously. It was the first section I would turn to, to see what happened that week. It was through the Sonoma Police report that I could see just how odd and funny people could be, including locals and visitors.

None of this is to take away from the seriousness of a police officer's job or the importance of deterring crime. But there's crime, and then there's "Oh My God did you see the police report today" . . . This book is about that: the funny, the odd, the twisted, the bizarre, the ludicrous and the borderline obscene. A glimpse of Sonoma provided by it's rowdiest locals, a glimpse of Sonoma you're not going to get from Sunset Magazine. So pull a cork on a wine bottle, pour a glass, and have a laugh!

RUN! RUN! RUN!

My friend and I were walking down East Napa Street one day and a police car passed us. We decided to run. Because we were bored. Sure enough they flipped a U-turn and chased us for a few blocks, lit us up, and of course, caught us. We couldn't catch our breath because we were laughing so hard. "What's so funny? Why were you running?" they asked. "We just wanted to see what you would do!" we replied. They didn't find this funny. Matter of taste. Here are some more stories of people running through the valley.

A shirtless man wearing a baseball cap was spotted leaping fences in the area of West Spain Street and First Street West late Tuesday.

An emu was seen running loose on Broadway, south of Leveroni Street Friday morning. Police found the emu in a nearby field.

A worried mother called police later Wednesday to report that her son had been chased by a man wearing pink in-line skates.

It was dusk moving into night, and we had been up at Lake Berryessa all day. We were coming back on Highway 121, into Sonoma, right past the county line. We noticed these lines and lines of people along the road and were wondering, "what the hell is going on here?" Then I realized this was the night they were going to run with the Olympic torch from Napa through Sonoma, and onward on 121. All of these people had shown up early to get a spot and were waiting for the torch. My buddy had a Chevelle. So we pulled over and started talking. He wanted to run with the torch. I said, "The hell with it, I'll drive," because I wasn't drunk. We took a stick and wrapped it up with a bunch of socks and we dipped it in gas or something like that, so it would burn. We put something on top of the car to make it official, a spotlight. So he got out in front of the car, lit torch in hand, and ran, in his shorts, probably his swimsuit, with no shirt and I followed in the car driving slowly behind him with the light on. All these people are cheering and yelling, "Yay! Yay! Here comes the Olympic torch! There it is! There it is!" When actually it was just a few stupid teenagers. We probably drove a ¼ to ½ a mile before we turned off and headed into town. The next day, my mom overheard that we had been arrested, but we were never caught.

-Dave, local

DRIVER RUNS, BUT CALLED OUT AT HOME

A 77-year-old Boyes Hot Springs man was arrested on suspicion of driving under the influence Tuesday, after a deputy finally pulled the man over in front of his home. Tom Oaks of Temple Avenue was seen by the arresting deputy traveling south on Highway 12 in his Chevrolet pickup. The deputy reported that Oaks turned left onto Ruta Avenue in front of an oncoming car, which was able to stop in time to avoid a crash. The pickup continued on Ruta after stalling briefly, and turned right on Temple, going through a stop sign at the intersection with Ruta. While Oaks was on Temple, he attempted to turn into his driveway but missed, striking a power pole. He then backed up and pulled into his driveway, parking on the sidewalk in front of his home. When approached by the deputy, Oaks claimed the officer could not arrest him since he had made it to his driveway without hitting anyone. The deputy then pointed out that he ran into the power pole, which Oaks denied.

> *If you were running from the cops on foot it was usually pretty easy. You could just jump in a bush and not move and they'd get tired of searching for a bunch of kids in the bushes and take off.*
>
> *-Brian, local*

Just before 2 am Monday, someone was spotted running across the roof of a Plaza restaurant.

A juvenile, about 12 years old, ran into a local deli last week, grabbed a 12-pack of beer, threw $7 and hightailed it for the door. The only other description given was "fast shoes."

> *We roll up on this car parked in the middle of an intersection with the lights on and engine running. There is this guy, Will Augeson, passed out in the car, with the widows rolled up. So I decide to run in place and tap on the window. I start running in place and tapping, saying, Will! Will! Will, stop the car! Will, stop the car! Please stop the car! He wakes up and looks at me, panicked and slams on the breaks of his already parked car. I stop running. He rolls down the window and I say, "What are you doing, man? I've been chasing you forever." He was pretty drunk and disoriented. Well, when we transported him up north, the transporting officer asked him what*

happened, and he said, "Well, I dunno. There was a cop running next to me knocking on the window, yelling at me to stop and so I did." The transporting officer looked at me with an odd expression, and I just shrugged my shoulders like I had no idea what he was talking about.

-Officer Clayton, Sonoma Police

Officers received several calls Sunday afternoon about a bull "running amok" near the intersection of Fifth Street East and East Napa Street. But when officers responded, they found that the bull's owner already had captured the rather tame-appearing bull and was leading him back to his herd in a nearby field.

The cops would cuff and stuff people, put them in the car and go back to get other people. One night at a party, they cuff and stuffed Jim and went back to get more people. We snuck up to the police car and Jim is yelling at us, "Open the door. Open the door." So we simply opened the door, he jumped out of the car and we took off running. Never got popped for that.

-Jared, local

The photographer for the Sonoma Index Tribune was taking pictures of firemen fighting a local kitchen fire, when the 60-year-old homeowner attacked him with a fire extinguisher, chasing him down the street and attempting to grab his camera. The photographer placed the woman under citizen's arrest.

Some of the drivers have people run on them. That's why I wear my Jordans. The dispatcher will usually give you a heads up if the person sounds sketchy and is going to Petaluma or Santa Rosa, so you can be prepared for the chase.

-Al, cabbie

Lefner Road residents said there was a man, attired only in his skivvies, running down the street. They also heard a gunshot. The man told deputies someone was trying to shoot him. Witnesses said the man in his underwear was the one with the gun. Deputies found a .22 caliber rifle in the area but no one would claim ownership.

We were pretty loaded at a bar out in El Verano. And Tim, who is pretty cheap, didn't want to take a cab back into town, so we decided we would walk the few miles into town. We start stumbling back to town, and we pass this magnolia tree. I pick a couple of big flowers off it and put [them] in my pocket. I also had a harmonica in my other pocket. A **"He feels the bulge in my pocket, maybe thinking it's a sack of weed and he says, "What's this?!" And pulls out the little bunch of magnolia flowers."** *cop car drives past us, and Tim decides to take off running, for no reason. He disappears through the bushes, and the cop turns around and stops me on the side of the road. The cop starts interviewing me and grilling me, wondering who I was with and wanting to know why Tim started running. I told him I just met the guy and didn't know his name. The cop didn't believe me. So after a bit, he says, "We're going to give you a ride home, but we have to frisk you first." One of the cops was cool and the other was pretty high-strung and amped up. The high-strung one starts to frisk me and asks me if I have any weapons on me. I tell him no, and he says, "Oh yeah, then what's this?!!" He whips out my harmonica. Stares at if for a second and then asks me if I have any drugs on me as he continues to frisk me. I say, "No sir." He feels the bulge in my pocket, maybe thinking it's a sack of weed, and he says, "What's this?!" And pulls out the* *little bunch of magnolia flowers. And his partner starts laughing. They eventually gave me a ride home. Turns out, Tim was 12 feet away the entire time hiding in a bush. He thought the whole thing was pretty funny.*

-Otis, local

The escape of a prisoner, whom frustrated deputies believe might possess world class Olympic Games speed, was also reported here on Friday, July 6, at about 8:45 p.m. The escapee, identified as Roberto Marini, 22, Sonoma, clad only in blue swim trunks, was allowed to make a telephone call, and while not handcuffed and the deputies were momentarily going over a report, he ran out the front door and fled across a nearby field. He was chased by two deputies, who eventually lost sight of him.

YOU LOOK STUNNING

Runway models these are not. Most criminals wear ski masks, dark clothes, and plan to look inconspicuous. It seems that these Sonomans just can't deny their style.

A pair of subpoena servers caused some consternation on Cavedale Road on Monday. Callers reported two men dressed in camouflage fatigues, jungle boots, and black facial paint. Both were armed with rifles, handguns in cross-draw holsters, and "mini" 14's. Sheriff's deputies tracked down the men, who turned out to be process servers. The servers, according to sheriff's deputies, were polite and cooperative. The reason for their unusual dress, they told deputies, was that they were afraid of coming across "dope growers" en route to serve a civil subpoena to a valley man.

> *"Officer Dummy." That's what they called him. It was a dummy that they dressed as a cop and put in an extra police car. They would take the car and leave it around town at intersections where people were speeding. It was supposedly pretty effective.*
> *-Stanley, local*

A Pike Drive resident reported that every morning between 9 and 10 a.m. a man with gray hair and beard, wearing green pants and a straw hat, rides his bicycle to a telephone pole near the resident's house, stops, dismounts, looks around and then urinates on the pole, after which he looks around again and rides off on his bike. Police later witnessed the man in action and spoke with him.

A guy wearing pink pants was seen peering into cars on Joaquin Drive late Saturday.

This guy told the cops that one of the cabbies robbed him. But the guy was in a full clown outfit. Nobody believed him. The guy was not all there, a little crazy.

-Kevin, cabbie

ONE STRANGE BIRD CAGED
A man wearing women's clothing was arrested for trespassing in Glen Ellen Sunday night after two residents on Lennon Drive reported he was harassing them at their homes. A woman reported that a man wearing a yellow shirt, black skirt, high heels, make-up and a dark wig showed up on her porch. The woman said the man had followed her home from the Glen Ellen Market, and was acting strangely and making a "statement" about communicating with birds." She asked him to leave, and he did, but he returned an hour later. She told him again to leave again and he did. After he left the second time, the woman walked over to a friend's house. The man showed up there, as well, and that's when the friend's husband called for police. Deputies arrived and contacted the man. They found four hypodermic needles in his backpack. They also searched his car, where they found another wig, more women's clothing, and a trumpet.

A WOODEN SWORD AND PIRACY IN THE PLAZA
She did not have an eye patch, a parrot or a wooden leg, but she did have a wooden sword and either the dream, the hope or the besotted illusion of being a pirate. There is no evidence in the police report that 24-year-old Liz Shapiro, a resident of San Mateo, said words like

"Aaarrrrgghh," "Shiver me timberrrs," "Avast!," or "Bucko." But she did reportedly use some unprintable salutations before wielding her pirate sword in the Plaza around 6:30 p.m. on March 30. It all began when Shapiro and her boyfriend, a 26-year-old Sonoman, had commenced to consume considerable portions of some powerful potion, though there is no evidence that their beverage of choice was rum. They nevertheless managed, police reported, to become sufficiently intoxicated to lower the plank on their emotions. The boyfriend became embroiled in a bout of what police called, "mutual combat" with a third member of the party. As **"Shiver me Timberrrs, Avast!!"** the two men struggled, Shapiro lifted the wooden sword and smote the third party on the head hard enough to split the sword asunder. Police were summoned and arrived in time to find the assaulted one with a blood-covered face, a two-inch gash on his forehead in need of stitches, along with a sizeable goose egg. Police asked Shapiro, "Why the sword?" "Because," explained Shapiro, "I'm a pirate."

BE ON THE LOOKOUT FOR A THIEF IN A TUTU
Deputies will be on the lookout today for a thief dressed as a ballerina after the pink dancing costume was stolen Friday afternoon. A resident of Boyes Hot Springs told deputies that the fluffy attire was taken from an unlocked car parked in the 18600 block of Highway 12.

> *Make-up. We get more women's make-up stolen than any other item in the store. It used to be condoms. That was because some young kids are just too embarrassed to buy them. You understand and feel bad about it.*
>
> *-Jacob, store security*

A man with scraggly hair and a Fu Manchu mustache short-changed a clerk at the Vineyard Deli Sunday.

There was an Italian marching band in the Fourth of July parade one year, and they couldn't keep a tune, couldn't stay in line, they were all over the place, wandering into the crowds and into the pubs. That was their gag. They were quite funny!

-Ray, local

Police are looking for a well-groomed thief who stole manicuring equipment and a heating lamp from a beauty salon on East Napa Street, Wednesday.

Two women and one man described by employees of the Ranch House Restaurant as "looking like Gypsies" reportedly grabbed $140 from the restaurant's register and ran last Thursday evening. The trio apparently worked as a team, one grabbing the money, while one held the door open, while the third drove the get-away car, described as a tan or brown station wagon. Employees of the Mexican restaurant on Broadway said the three ranged from 40 to 60 years old, dressed in colorful clothing, wore a great deal of jewelry, and offered to read fortunes for some of the employees.

There was a group of Sonomans that would dress up in capes and masks and promote Sonoma wine in various ways. They heard that Richard Branson, this very famous billionaire, was going to be coming to the wine country with a big entourage and was planning to spend the entire time in Napa Valley. They thought that was bullshit, so they some- **"Sonomans that would dress** *how got a* **up in capes and masks."** *hold of the billionaire's people without him knowing, and they staged a fake high-jacking of his bus when it was on its way to Napa. They redirected the bus to Sonoma, where they poured a bunch of Sonoma wine. They hung out for a while drinking and having a good time, and then they sent them off to Napa.*

-David, local

VANDAL TRASHES TRIXI

Sebastiani Theatre mannequin loses precious knickknacks. Trixie, the mute mannequin that has for years greeted moviegoers from the ticket booth of the Sebastiani Theatre, had a terrifying experience Tuesday night when an unknown vandal broke through the back panel of her booth. Just as she reached for the phone to notify authorities, the assailant ripped her antique telephone from off the wall and made off with all of her precious knickknacks. "Everything, the monster took everything," said the mannequin in an unconfirmed report. "They even took my vintage medicine bottles." With no phone, Trixie was forced to wait motionless for the rest of the night until the Assistant Manager came in Wednesday morning to find the damage. "I looked at Trixie, and her glasses were askew," she said. "It looks like they roughed her up a little bit." Unfortunately for Trixie, this is not the first time someone has broken into her booth. Around a year ago, another goon broke through the glass of the booth and made off with a few tchotchkes. "We would like to think that this is a small town and things like that don't happen here," said the manager of the theater. This time, whoever broke in made off with everything but Trixie herself. The booth, once full of colorful objects, is now bare. Most of the stolen items were antique medicine bottles, make-up, small toys and - most notably - a vintage telephone. Most of the baubles belonged to the theater projectionist, who supplied the pieces for the enjoyment of the community. The thief also made off with a collection of photocopied autographed pictures of movie stars. The value of the stolen items is unknown.

Trixie got stolen from the Sebastiani Theatre. A few days later someone found her and returned her. She is the most photographed thing in Sonoma. She's a mannequin in a booth.

-Anderson, local

A 59-year-old Sonoma man with a penchant for eye makeup and bronzing skin lotion picked up some skin products, purchased a cup of coffee and then sat down in the lounge area of Sonoma Market. There he sipped while applying the products to his face, then put some in his pocket, others in a black valise, went back to the soda cooler, paid for a cold drink at the register, but not the eye beautification and skin toning products, and exited the store. The market's loss prevention officer stopped the man outside, questioned him about the products in his pocket, at which point the shoplifter replied, "Oh alright, I'll give them back." Apparently the LPO did not ask the most compelling question, i. e., "What's up with the face tint?" Total value of the products was more than $100. The man was cited for petty theft and released.

About 3:40 a.m. yesterday morning deputies said they clocked a gold Cadillac at 90 mph along Arnold Drive and gave chase before the driver lost control on Sobre Vista Drive, stopped the car and fled on foot. The driver turned out to be Joel Milla, a prison parolee, who exited the car and ran off in his "bunny slippers" before deputies apprehended him.

We were able to avoid the police for most of our escapades in capes and masks.

-Gary, local

THEY'RE ACTING LIKE ANIMALS

When I was a kid the plaza was full of functional community businesses. Food City, the Bus Depot, Pinelli's Mission Hardware, Pete's Electric, and the Feed store. The Feed store sold all kinds of animal fodder, because back in the day, Sonomans raised all kinds of animals. There is still a pretty eclectic mix of animals in the wine country.

RELEASED ON HIS OWN "REFROGNIZANCE"

Last week it was a bull. This week it was a bullfrog that Sonoma Police officers were called on to subdue. In the end, they had better luck with the bull. A resident of Strong Street called the station last Tuesday complaining of "strange, low noises" coming from the field behind her home. The source of these noises, officers discovered, was a bullfrog calling to his ladylove across the field. When told the source of the noise, the woman demanded the officers shoot the romantic frog. Not wanting to mess with Mother Nature or, for that matter, the City Fathers, the officers explained to the woman that it was against the law to discharge a firearm inside the city. Kermit and friend are free on their own "refrognizance."

One night out at YO's Triangle, (that's the split at the fire station in Schellville), one of our deputies, a really gruff guy, sees a car pulled over to the side of road. This is late, after the bars had closed. Well, there's a guy there taking a whiz and the deputy gets out of the car, yelling at him, asking what he was doing and telling him to get on his way. The guy says, "I'm sorry officer, I just stopped to let my kangaroo out." The deputy says, "Well, get your kangaroo back in and get the bleep out of here." The guy whistles, and up pops a kangaroo out of the bushes. Hop, hop, hop right into the car, and they drove off. That officer was pretty shook up. We found out later, there was this fella who lived on the outskirts of town and worked for the San Francisco Zoo. I can't remember his name. Anyways he raised kangaroos; taught them how to ride bicycles and so forth.

-Officer Gregerson, Sonoma Police

An employee of a winery reported a deer with a red collar in a new vineyard off Fourth Street East. The reporting person was wrong. The connoisseur enjoying Sunday brunch was a goat (could it be cited for impersonating a deer?...) The tan and white female goat with red collar and broken horn was taken to a kennel.

On Thursday afternoon, June 21, employees of Gasser Cable TV called the cops, noting that a bird resembling one in a potato chip commercial was in their yard. The gallivanting but friendly fowl was incarcerated at the city kennels and later adopted by a local farm family.

It was 3 in the morning, and I was coming down East Napa Street and there were all these motorcycles stopped. I pulled up, and it was a bunch of Hells Angels, and one of the Hells Angels had gotten bitten by a raccoon. They asked me if I could escort them to the hospital. So two of **"One of the Hells Angels had got bitten."** *them on bikes followed me to the hospital, and the rest of the Angels went down to the Sonoma Bowl and waited.*

-Officer Thomas, Sonoma Police

FEARLESS DEPUTY FINDS 8-FOOT BOA CONSTRICTOR SUNBATHING

It's encouraging to know that the sheriff's deputies are prepared for any emergency-even snakes. Deputies were called out on reports that a boa constrictor had gotten loose in a yard on Regal Circle in Agua Caliente Monday afternoon. The responding deputy was well prepared and undaunted by possible danger to himself. "If the snake eats me, I'll still be able to communicate with you- I have my portable radio on," he told the radio dispatcher. But the 8-foot-long pet snake turned out to be lying in the sun under the watchful eye of its owner. Apparently the heater in the snake's terrarium was malfunctioning, and the snake, who is susceptible to colds, was just staying warm.

Officers were called to Benson Street late Wednesday after a man reported that his neighbor's cat got his head stuck in an Alpo can. The owner was concerned the head was starting to swell. Officers wrapped the cat in a towel and yanked the can off his relieved little head.

The owner of the theater came into the store one day and said, "Bring your shotgun over to the theater tomorrow." I said, "O.K." So I show up with my gun, and I guess pigeons had been messing up his marquee and such and he was tired of it. So I get set across the street in front of the theater and Joe Marras gets on the library steps (now the Visitors Bureau) with his shotgun. The Chief of Police is directing traffic so nobody could come down 1st street. And we started shooting our guns. I think **"Bring your shotgun over to the theatre tomorrow."** *we only killed 3 pigeons, but I was afraid we were going to end up in Santa Rosa in jail and the chief as well!*

-Tom, local

An anonymous person reported to police on June 19 at 8:07 p.m. that an adult male on the city bike path near the Depot Museum had a live rattlesnake in a bag.

For a while people would come in here and ask, "Who serves Turtle soup?" It was pretty **"Who serves Turtle Soup?"** *confusing until we figured out that there was a restaurant in town that was serving Turtle soup on the menu.*

-Max, local

A pet raccoon that resides on East Napa Street was missing Monday morning, it was reported. The owner said his masked friend, who was last seen wearing a pink collar, is very friendly and may approach anyone she comes in contact with.

The lady who called to report a possum in a trap placed in her yard, gave an erroneous I.D. The varmint was a skunk, which police transported, at arm's length, into the hills behind town.

When they closed the old dump up here, above town, the rats took over the town. Thousands of them! It was a rat invasion. They closed the dump, and the rats had nothing to eat, so **"Thousands of them! It was a rat invasion."** *they came down the ditch, past the Vet's Building, into town. They were everywhere. So we had to put poison out to kill them all.*

-Officer Thomas, Sonoma Police

"Bunny on Board" might have to be the new sign carried by Sonoma officers on the early morning shift, as Cpl. Jim Volte picked up his second French "lop" rabbit in less than a week early Thursday morning. This one, dubbed "Gigi" by the officers, is now keeping "Maurice," the rabbit picked up last week, company in the department's kennel.

Deputies responded to a call this weekend of a prowler in the 2000 block of Muletz Road. Upon arrival, they found the culprits to be four deer and one "unusually large" bullfrog. No arrest were made because deputies "didn't have a pair of cuffs to fit any of them," the report said.

Judy Lathan reported a giant turtle in her front yard Saturday morning. Police captured and released the beast.

A resident of Plymouth Drive reported that some "big, fat" peacocks were roaming her yard and hopping on her roof Tuesday. The feathered trespassers were reportedly pecking at the decorative plastic flamingos in the yard.

FOUND PET RAT AWAITS LOST OWNER
A "very friendly, king-sized rat" was found Tuesday afternoon in the area of Seventh Street West in Sonoma and is patiently awaiting its owner at a local pet shop. "It's well-fed and looks very nice," said

29

a community service officer with the Sonoma Police department. "It'll just climb into your hand; it's definitely someone's pet." The rat, described as a white female with a brown head, is being held without bail at Little Rascals Pet Supplies on West Napa Street.

A man called the valley substation Thursday morning to complain that a pit bull was lurking around his Schellville home, attempting to visit his female dog, who happened to be in heat. He said he had already called the Sonoma County Animal Control Department and now wanted officers to come down and shoot the pesty dog. They said no.

A Carolyn Circle resident called police to report that an opossum was stuck in his fence. Officers liberated the little guy and let him loose in some nearby vineyards.

> We used to take the skunks up to the old dumps, up on Norrbom Road, right above town. I shot one or two up there. We'd dispose of 'em at that time.
> -Officer Jenkins, Sonoma Police

California Highway Patrol told officers that there was a large fire with 10-foot flames on West Spain Street and Fourth Street West late Saturday. Sonoma Fire Department was sent to investigate. They learned that a steer was being barbecued.

GREASY CAT SPARKS NEIGHBORHOOD FEUD

Two Fairview Court neighbors got into an argument Thursday after one accused the other of dipping his cat in oil. Police went to the street and found the two residents who were involved in a heated disagreement there. Following a brief investigation, officers determined that the cat was at fault-it knocked an uncovered can of oil on itself.

The department couldn't get rid of this officer, so they made him the animal control officer. I had set some traps in the back of the house to protect my ducks. I caught a skunk in one of the cages, and I call him, and he comes over. It's a big skunk, and I ask him what we should do. He says, "I'm not going after that thing." He tells me, "The best you can do is shoot the skunk yourself." So I grabbed my .22 and shot the skunk, and he got a stick and removed it. He wasn't much of an animal control officer.

-Ray, local

NEIGHBORS BAFFLED BY ODD ANIMAL WITH LONG NOSE

Sonoma Police received calls from homeowners on First Street West Saturday morning. They were concerned about a small, brown animal that was roaming their neighborhood. They described the trespasser as having a long nose and a tail. The mysterious beast also made a snorting sound, they said. First Street West residents are still wondering what the heck it was. Police theorized it was an anteater.

We had the locals who would come down [to the Plaza] with their dogs, and they were drinking beer. You know, they always have a local crowd in the rose garden. And they would bring their dogs down, and the dogs would start attacking the ducks. And then we'd have people, who were coming in to visit the town, that would bring their dogs, and they would have them off-leash and that became a problem. So now there's no dogs allowed in the Plaza.

-Officer Jenkins, Sonoma Police

The owner of two German shepherds named "Frankie" and "Harry" called police to say that the dogs had gotten away and were heading toward town Thursday night.

FERRET CAUGHT IN FAMILY FIGHT

Sonoma police discovered that a ferret named Slinky was illegally living in a Valley home Saturday. Officers, who found the sly little European polecat running around the house with a dachshund, confiscated the animal- which is illegal in this state- and took it to a refuge area. The owners were ticketed.

> One day, I was working the restaurant; waiting tables outside on the back deck of La Casa because we were short-handed. My one table kept complaining about the flies. At one point, the customer said to me, "Can't you do something about these **"Sir, these are not our flies."** flies?" I turned to him and said, "Sir, these are not our flies, they are from the El Dorado Hotel, and are just here having lunch."
>
> -Bill, local

Two birds and a birdcage were stolen from the front porch of a home on Thurber Lane Tuesday. One was a gray and peach cockatiel, the other a blue parakeet. According to the owner, both birds could whistle the Polish national anthem and another Polish song, and could say "Hello, Peaches." The birds are worth $165 each.

ONE-EARED STEER SNATCHED

A 34-year-old woman on Carriger Road reported someone may have stolen her steer. The woman said she returned home to find her steer missing from its pasture, which is guarded by a password-activated security gate. A deputy responded and found no evidence of tampering with the gate, and confirmed the steer- which has a white face and is missing its right ear- was nowhere to be found. The deputy could not determine at the time if the animal was in fact the victim of a cattle rustler, or whether the steer escaped on its own.

My favorite drunk was Miles O'Connor. He was so famous in Glen Ellen that he ran against my dog for election. My dog was really famous in Glen Ellen as well. So we had a mock election to see which would be appointed mayor.

-Seth, local

An El Verano woman called deputies requesting they take a "non-stinking" skunk out of a trap near her home. The case was referred to the county's Animal Regulation Department.

THE INCREDIBLE JOURNEY—OVER AND OVER AGAIN

In the absence of a common language, police were unable to successfully question a Verano Avenue Husky whose name, inexplicably, did not make it into the police report. There was no clear motive, therefore, to explain why the dog preferred doing time in jail than in the backyard of his actual home.

Here's how it went down. At some point the pooch effected an escape from his home confinement, reportedly through a hole in the family fence, and was running at large until animal control encountered and captured him, which meant confinement in the cushy kennel maintained by the police department at the edge of the Field of Dreams.

The police report does not describe the menu served at the detention kennel, but maybe it was alluring enough to inspire another escape because after the dog was claimed by its 25-year-old owner (who had to pay a $30 impound fee), it showed up the next day in front of the police station, apparently waiting for another free meal.

It was once again impounded, once again reclaimed for (once again) a $30 impound fee, and once again it returned the next day to the Sonoma police station. On July 18, for the third day in a row, the dog appeared at the police station, apparently convinced that the cop kennel with its canine cuisine was the best place to hang. When police called the mother of the owner to inquire how and why the great escape kept taking place, she told them her son had finally fixed the hole in the fence. The dog was retrieved again ($30 fine) and, at last report, had not reappeared at the police station, although only time will tell. Because, hey, it's always hard to keep a good dog down.

> *When the officers were bored, we'd go up Norrbom Road, you know, on the way to Mission Highlands, and shoot skunks out the window with our service revolvers.*
>
> *-Officer Flynn, Sonoma Police*

WOMAN FOUND SLEEPING AT CHICKEN CAR WASH WITH DEER

When Sonoma police received a complaint about some "suspicious circumstances" Nov. 26, possibly involving a person occupying a camper shell behind a building at a car wash, they had no way of knowing who or what they would find inside. When they responded to the call around 9 p.m., they discovered a row of long-parked camping shelters, including an old trailer and the camper shell in which the person in question was reportedly ensconced.

Peering through the evening gloom into the dim interior of the cramped space, police spotted a woman lying on a mattress, unresponsive and apparently unconscious. But before they could determine her condition, they also noticed some sort of body on the floor of the structure and retreated to assess the situation, not wanting to crawl across whatever it was in the dark. A call to the car wash owner clarified that the body was, in fact, that of a deer, but that it had been stuffed many years before, and was a gift he had stored in the trailer. And at this point, it was very dead. Returning to the camper shell, police climbed over the deer and managed to awaken 30-year-old Kathy Lassen of Santa Rosa. Beside Lassen, police discovered two white pills of a powerful and highly-addictive sedative called Lorazepam, lacking any prescription, along with a hypodermic syringe, and two rounds of .22 caliber ammunition. Lassen was arrested and booked into the county jail for felony possession of a controlled substance, but she was not charged with trespassing or poaching a dead deer.

We were at the old station next to the old firehouse on Patten Street, and on summer nights the door to the station would be wide open. We're sitting behind the counter dispatching, and a dog comes wandering in, a nice looking German shorthair. I looked at his tags and saw who it belonged to. I let him in behind the desk and he spent the night there.

-Officer Reed, Sonoma Police

IS THAT A BOA IN YOUR POCKET, OR?

Courageous police officers responded to a home on Andrieux Street after a resident reported spotting a large serpent in his yard. The stalwart officers arrived to discover that a 5-foot, brown and tan male boa constrictor had crawled under a backyard shed. Employing skills not taught at the POST academy, the officers somehow coaxed the wily reptile out of hiding and turned it over to a reptile rescuer in Sebastopol.

Our dog would always get out of the yard and head down to the Plaza. He'd go straight to the pond with fish in it in front of City Hall. They would either call us, or the guys who worked in the park would throw him in their truck and bring him back to our place.

-Phillip, local

The manager of the Sonoma Hotel called police to report having a turtle in custody after finding it strolling down the street in front of the hotel. Police took it into custody and released it into Sonoma Creek.

NAKED IN THE VALLEY OF THE MOON

I guess I shouldn't be too surprised that people are running around Sonoma naked. People used to come up here for a century to soak (presumably naked) in the hot springs. Free love and nakedness was only a stone's throw away in San Francisco and there has always been bohemian vibe about Sonoma...But there's naked, and then there's Police Report naked...

About 9:30 p.m. Wednesday, a woman called to report an unidentified male "in his birthday suit" riding a bicycle. She said the male Lady Godiva was last seen coming out of Olsen Park headed toward Linda Drive.

> *There was a troupe coming to perform in town. Well, we found out that they perform in the nude. There was a lot of drama with the police. They had a show at the Community Center. They were coming down the street naked. It was cold as hell. Everyone was naked except for one guy in his underwear.*
>
> *-Phillip, local*

UNCLOTHED RUNNER ARRESTED

A naked woman, reported running down the center of a Glen Ellen street last week, was taken into custody on public drunkenness charges. Sheriff deputies apprehended the 30-year-old female, wearing nothing but a smile, on Billingsley Road on Tuesday. Some 15 hours later, deputies found the Glen Ellen woman in the same drunken condition. She was taken into custody on the same charge. This time however, officers noted, she was clothed.

There is some truth to this story. Although I do not believe that it hit the police blotter, but the cops did show up. The story goes back to the 60's when my Dad used to play on the square, and the bet was "I bet you can't run around the Plaza in just one shoe." And that literally was just one shoe and nothing else. Tim and I knew about this bet, and it was around my birthday many years ago. Tim and I had been celebrating all day and we finally got to the Swiss after stop-offs at La Casa, Murphy's, Town Square and the old Steiners. We were sitting out front and I said to him, "I bet you can't run around the Plaza in just one shoe." Next thing you know, we are stripping down, and we take off run-ning in opposite directions. I go

"The next thing you know, we are stripping down."

down Spain to First Street West, and he heads east on Spain headed for First Street East. People start coming out of Piatti and various establishments on the Plaza and are cheering us on. I fly by Tim on the Eastern part of the City Hall Horseshoe, and as we pace I am in the lead. Note that my balls are killing me because there is no support, but the laughter makes it all better. People are hollering and laughing as I fly up First Street East, and I get back to The Swiss just before my brother. We are sweating and out of breath, but we hear the cops are coming. We get dressed out front of The Swiss and just as we are sitting down for another cold beer, the cops show up. Larry the Legend is behind the bar at the Swiss doing his thing, and he is aware of the footrace and knows the sprinters. But when the cops show up and start asking questions, he covers for the young lads and sends the cops down the street looking for two non-descript subjects. As the cops come down the steps of the bar at The Swiss, they ask us if we have seen any naked runners, and we say that we have been sitting here for hours and haven't seen a thing. Sweat rolling down our faces and condensation rolling down our beers. One shoe.

-*Jason, local*

NAKED MAN CLAIMS HE'S JESUS

Officers received a report of a suspicious character on Arnold Drive just after midnight Sunday. The responding deputy found a man standing naked in the road. When the deputy asked the man who he was, the man responded that he was Jesus Christ.

Man in orange socks found walking down middle of street. At one point in time that was the worst crime there was.

-*Phillip, local*

Juveniles in the area of Walnut Avenue were reported to be "mooning" people, but they were gone by the time deputies arrived.

They don't call it Valley of the Moon for nothing.

-*Kevin, local*

NAKED CAME THE STRANGER

It was 2:21 a.m., Tuesday, March 16, in the middle of an otherwise peaceful Sonoma night when a police officer on patrol in his squad car spotted a pedestrian who crossed West Mac-Arthur Street in front of him and disappeared down the bike path beside Fryer Creek. Not quite convinced his eyes weren't deceiving him, the officer pulled up and shone his spotlight down the path. Sure enough, there was the man he'd seen, out for an incongruous early-morning stroll, completely naked. No clothes. No shoes. He was, as the British say, starkers. The officer exited the car to investigate the strange apparition. The man ducked behind a bush; the officer demanded he come out, and he did, his condition obviating the need for any kind of body search. Asked what he was doing, the man apologized profusely several times and explained that he was simply "very hot." The officer ordered the naked stranger to his knees and placed handcuffs on his wrists, then examined him for signs of intoxication or drug use. The man's mouth was dry and his eyes were red, but he had no other objective signs of being under the influence of anything, except perhaps heat. "I was very hot," he explained again, "So I decided to go for a walk." The officer administered a preliminary breath test to determine if the man had been drinking, but his blood alcohol level registered exactly zero. The man told the officer he lived nearby with three roommates, so after citing him for disorderly conduct, he drove the man to his house where, it turned out, he had a wife. The wife explained that her husband had been sleeping upstairs while she slept on the first floor with other family members, and she didn't know he was gone. She said he was not taking any medications and an inspection of the house revealed no drugs of any kind. He was just, it seems, very hot. The naked wayfaring stranger was cited and released.

There was a nude sunbathing group up near Buena Vista.
-Anderson, local

I found this couple "doing it" behind the shopping center in a car. I shined the light in the car and told them to knock it off, and they fumbled around and just drove off... naked. They **"They just drove off buck naked."** *didn't even take the time to put their clothes back on. They just drove off buck naked in the car.*

-Officer Hamil, Sonoma Security

Deputies were called to Bonnie Road Sunday evening after receiving a report that a naked man was dancing in the street. There they found a fully-dressed man wearing an auburn wig, black tights, a trench coat, high heels, "tons" of makeup **"Naked man dancing in the street."** and a set of falsies. In addition, several sexual devices were lying on the ground nearby, they said. He told them he was "cavorting with nature." Deputies, noting he did not reside in the Valley, told him to pack up his gear and go home.

There was a ranch resort just outside of town that was clothing-optional. The postman, and the UPS man, would deliver there; they'd take off their clothes and go for a swim. Pick up some chicks. Stay as long as they could and then go back to work.

-Anderson, local

Two people were spotted "intertwined" in Mountain Cemetery Saturday afternoon.

I was pretty new [to the taxi service], and I picked her up at the Swiss Hotel. And this girl gets in the backseat, and she was out of it, really drunk. And I'm heading up to her neighborhood and she's going on about stuff, but she

can't figure out where the place is. She climbs over the seat to the front of the cab, looking out the window. Then she starts taking all her clothes off, everything. She's stark naked. It's 4:30 p.m. It's light out. It was weird as hell. I'm just driving back and forth on this road looking for the house. Finally, she started putting her clothes on, she's half dressed as I see this older man in a driveway. Well-dressed, respectable. I pull over to ask him if he can help us find a house, and he looks in and sees her. Runs around and opens the door and yanks her out. It was her dad. He was pissed as hell.

-Kevin, cabbie

LOOSE PANTS FOIL PRUNER

A man who brandished a pair of pruning shears at an officer Thursday afternoon was taken into custody after the man reached to prevent his pants from falling down. The officer responded to an indecent exposure call on Highway 12 and located a man in the roadway at the intersection of Highway 12 and Ramon Street. The officer said the man appeared intoxicated and had urinated on himself. The officer ordered the man out of the road and while trying to take him into custody, the man pulled out a pair of pruning shears from a sheath on his hip and began waving them at the officer. But when the man's pants began to fall down, he was obliged to reach down for them, and when he did so, the officer disarmed him and took him into custody.

There was a guy and a girl who requested the taxi van so they could get driven around town while they had sex in the van.

-Al, cabbie

A San Rafael man picked the wrong evening to party-or-what-ever-on Skaggs Island Road. A Sonoma County sheriff's deputy on patrol on Skaggs Island Road at around 8:55 p.m. Thursday, Nov. 29, found 43-year-old Dougald Beyer of San Leandro naked, slathered with petroleum jelly and smoking crack cocaine. Beyer, who also had prison tattoos, was cooperative and after getting dressed was arrested.

"Naked, slathered with petroleum jelly."

I was coming across Andrieux Street at Broadway. I didn't know who the guy was, but he was standing there in his jockey shorts. That's it. Just his underwear. It had to be 32 degrees outside, and he was standing there talking to a Sonoma Police officer. I don't know what happened, because it didn't make it into the police report.

-Barbara, local

SUNSCREEN ON A CLOUDY DAY?
Hmmm. Deputies responded to the parking lot at Maxwell Farms Regional Park on the report of a man exposing himself in a vehicle. While en route, deputies were informed that the victim didn't want to be involved with pressing charges. Upon arrival at the scene, deputies made contact with the motorist, a 45-year-old male from Sebastopol. The man denied he had exposed himself and said he was just sitting in his car doing some paperwork. Deputies noticed that, despite the rainy day, the man had installed a sunscreen across his windshield. The deputies also noticed the smell of marijuana and, after a search of the vehicle, cited the man for possession of marijuana in a vehicle.

They said he had had too much Chocolate. It made him take off all his clothes and run around the restaurant in the El Dorado Hotel completely naked. With customers dining there. He was a tall wiry guy and the bartender was this short heavyset guy. The bartender is chasing this guy all around the restaurant with a sheet in his hand trying to cover him up but he couldn't catch him. Must have been a pretty funny sight.

-Ash, local

HANDS AT 10 AND 2

People do weird things in cars. Nowadays you have people texting, sending emails, doing make-up, even watching t.v. shows. I was fortunate enough to learn a lesson early on in my life about driving. It is not wise to wave a fake gun around in a car. And it's really not wise if there is a 16 year-old girl next to you. I was 16 at the time and was coming home from summer school. Apparently, I was goofing around with her, laughing and being stupid with this cap gun. We were on Napa Road at 5th Street West when I noticed a cop behind me. I look down and see two more Sonoma Cops flying down 5th Street in my direction. No lights have been flipped on yet. I pull forward and as I'm heading over the bridge on Leveroni road I see three more cops coming east in my direction from Arnold Drive. That's when it all made sense. I crossed the bridge, pulled over into a pull-out and all six of the cars lit me up. I stopped the car, got out, turned around to explain "it's a cap gun" and I'm looking at every cop with their guns drawn, screaming at me to GET ON THE GROUND! GET ON THE GROUND! Which I did, pronto. They cuff me and stuff me in the back of one of the police cars while they talk to the girl. The girl is crying hysterically. Finally, when they find out that I was just driving her home from summer school, they let me go and told me to make sure my mom called the police station when I got home so they could tell her what I'd done. Now I realize I wasn't alone in questionable behavior behind the wheel.

IT MUST HAVE BEEN THE CELLOPHANE COMIC
A white man in his late 30's was spotted with a plastic bag tied over his head, banging himself against his black Cadillac about 5 p.m. Saturday in the Safeway parking lot. The woman who witnessed this said he was "hitting his back against the car," according to the police. When an officer arrived, the man explained that he was a stand-up comic, trying out a new routine on his family. But no family members were present in the car.

> *My dad had a work van that he bought for his one-man business. He put the number 238 on the back of it, so it would appear to be one of many and the company would appear bigger. Well, he gets back to his office one day, and this lady calls to complain. She said, "One of your drivers cut me off and flipped me off." He asked if she got the number of the van. She said, "The van number was 238." He told her not to worry, that that particular driver would be fired immediately, because that is not how his company does business. She said she didn't want him fired; she just thought the owner should know. He told her, "No, no. That's just not how we do business, ma'am."*
>
> *-Jeremy, local*

Deputies spotted what they said was a counterfeit license plate on a car parked in the lot of Sonoma National Golf Course Wednesday. The plate read: NITE RANGER. It was confiscated. Later, the owner of the vehicle, a 21-year-old resident of Vallejo, called the substation and insisted that his plate be returned. He said he was a fan of the rock-n-roll group Night Ranger and wanted members of the band to pose with him and his license plate. He didn't get his wish.

This is way back, when they put in the four stop signs on the Square. We came out of Parkside, a bar on the Square, jumped on our motorcycles and took off around the Square four times before one of the cops pulled us over. He said, "You know how many tickets I'm going to give you?" I said, "No." He said, "16. One for every stop sign you went through." They took me down to the police station and made me dry out.

-Eddie, local

Bank officials on Sonoma Highway were worried about a man in a red Camaro who was sitting in front of their business for more than two hours, Wednesday. Police chatted with the man who was "killing time reading comic books."

I drive around for a while, but it becomes clear the guy has no idea where he is, and the fare's too high. So I pull up to a cop, and say "This guy doesn't know where he's going and the fare's too high." Cop tells me, "Pull over, I know where he's going. How much does he owe you?" I tell him, "10 bucks." Cop says, "Let s make it 12 with a tip." So, the cop pays the fare and brings the guy to jail.

-Gordon, cabbie

Kristen Jean Lorry, 41, of Santa Rosa, was taken to Sonoma County jail after she was spotted riding around on the hood of a van and screaming at the driver in the Sonoma Police Department parking lot. The van's driver had sought police after apparently incurring Lorry's wrath during a traffic dispute. Lorry followed the van, and when the driver tried to leave the parking lot, Lorry jumped on the van's hood. After Lorry was placed under citizens' arrest, police searched her car and found a rusty steel rod, wrapped in duct tape, which Lorry had said she used for self-defense. She was booked for assault, vandalism, and possession of a deadly weapon.

One poor officer- the deputies liked to pick on him, because, boy, he would get so mad, but he was still a good guy, that's why they did things to him. The deputies would take the hubcaps off of the wheels on his car and put a handful of gravel in them- in the hubcaps- so when he'd take off the whole thing sounded like it was falling apart.

-Officer Reed, Sonoma Police

There was a report of a subject striking a driver with a liquid-filled balloon in the 200 block of West Napa Street. The balloon was believed to have contained orange soda.

We were partying in Petaluma, and we needed to get back to Sonoma. The Petaluma cabs said they were too busy to do it. Well, we get a hold of a cab in Sonoma and they agree to pick us up. They pick us up at East Washington and Petaluma Blvd. From there back to Sonoma, grab a pack of Marlboro Reds at 7-11 and get back in the cab... 8 minutes. The worst part of that is that was his second fastest time. He didn't break his own record. It was by far the only time I've put a seat belt on in a taxicab. When you're hammered and things are scary. You know that they really are scary!! 8 minutes from Petaluma to Sonoma. That's usually a 20-25 minute ride.

-Aaron, local

A man reported that he was driving on Boyes Boulevard at Riverside Drive and heard someone yell a threat about the man's wife. He happened to notice that his ex-wife was also driving down the **"She signaled a left hand turn "with the wrong finger."** street and he reported that she signaled a left-hand turn "with the wrong finger."

There's one regular that likes to go bar hopping to other towns. I'll drive him from town to town while he goes bar hopping: Cloverdale, Santa Rosa, Sebastapol, Cotati, and then back to Sonoma.

-Kevin, cabbie

Now, we just hang out in the horseshoe in front of City Hall around 1 a.m. Just our presence keeps people in line and helps encourage people to take a cab. It's made a difference.

-Officer Jenkins, Sonoma Police

An officer monitoring traffic at the Plaza, watched a silver Honda Civic make an illegal left turn from First Street West onto West Napa Street. When he contacted the driver and told him he had just made an illegal turn, the driver replied, "I'm from out of town. It's the only way I know to get back to my hotel." That led to a field sobriety test which included an eyes-closed exercise in nose touching with either hand. With one hand the driver repeatedly failed to find his nose with a finger, and with the second hand the officer caught him cheating as he tried to squint at his finger.

I've probably given out over 1,000 DUI's in my career. It's like shooting fish in a barrel.

-Officer Flynn, Sonoma Police

People that stay on the Plaza, at the little hotels there... like the Sonoma Hotel and the El Dorado Hotel, stuff like that, they go back to their room and they party 'til four or five in the morning. They get up at 7 o'clock to go out to breakfast, and they're still technically legally drunk.

-Officer Jenkins, Sonoma Police

AND IF THAT DOESN'T WORK, MOM WILL PAY

A San Francisco man who caught a taxi in the city to come up to Sonoma ended up in Santa Rosa - in jail. The man flagged down a taxi in San Francisco and bargained with the cabbie to reduce the usual $350 fare to $200. The cabbie sought assurance he'd be paid for the run, and the hopeful fare explained that he had a debit card, and if that didn't work, he had a credit card and if that didn't work his mother would pay. When the cab arrived at the mother's residence, the mother wanted nothing to do with her son or his $200 taxi fare. The cabbie called deputies and made a citizen's arrest on the 25-year-old San Francisco resident on charges of defrauding an innkeeper. Although the man was on the hook for the fare, he did receive a free ride to the county jail.

I was working at the firehouse, and we got dispatched to a vehicle accident on Highway 121 between Viansa Winery and the old Cherry Tree stand. We got on scene and found a lady had driven off the road and into a vineyard and taken out a bunch of vines and fencing. The lady wasn't hurt so the ambulance was cancelled, and we waited around for the tow truck to show. All of a sudden, the lady starts begging us to not call the cops, which I found interesting. We calmed this lady down and ask her why she didn't want the cops involved. Well, she had drunk a pint of vodka on her way up here from the East Bay. Turns out she is heading to the rehab place up valley, which she couldn't seem to remember the name of. My partner and I kind of get a kick out of it and decide to wait on scene until the cops show up, just to see what happens. The cop - a CHP- shows up and I pull him off to the side to tell him the story of what happened. All of a sudden the cop yells "F%*k!!" and slams his clipboard onto the ground. "This is so much

"Turns out she was heading to the rehab place up valley."

paperwork," he tells me. Turns out, this is the second one this week he has had to deal with. He had the same thing happen to him up on Highway 29 in St. Helena! Guess both of these people just wanted to have "one last party!"

-Aaron, local

There was a guy in town we would drive down to the city at 2 a.m. and we would drive around until he found a hooker. Then we would have to kill some time, pick him up afterwards, and drive him all the way back to Sonoma. That was a regular occurrence.

-Al, cabbie

Sonoma police spotted a truck with expired license plates and attempted a traffic stop when it pulled into a driveway on First Street West - the driveway, in fact, of the police station. The driver first straddled a curb, then attempted to back up and collided with a barrier, then attempted a three-point turn, when police stopped him. When they asked him for a driver's license, he handed them a credit card. The police ultimately found no record of his ever having owned a California driver's license. They did discover evidence of a felony, no-bail warrant for grand larceny. He was arrested on the warrant and for driving without a license and was booked into the county jail.

"When they asked him for a driver's license, he handed them a credit card."

"Do you know who you're dealing with?" You hear that a lot in this town. "Do you know who I am?" I say, "I could care less. You're breaking the law." "Do you know who my brother is? Do you know who my uncle is?" You break the law, you pay the price.

-Officer Hamil, Sonoma Security

51

HELLO, NEIGHBOR

It's a small town, no doubt. And I think that's most apparent in the neighborhood feel of Sonoma. People know their neighbors, people take care of each other, and sometimes a neighbor calls the police for some very interesting and odd things.

A family squabble was reported on Sonoma Highway on Sunday. Deputies found two newspaper carriers in a heated debate. It seems that the carriers are married and in happier times, the two would put the various sections of the paper together and deliver them. Now one is threatening to withhold the comics, thereby messing up the continuity of the newspaper. No arrests were made.

There was a tough older sheriff and a report of some trespassers around Arnold Drive and Leveroni Road. Well, he heads out there and finds these two guys on the property, fishing in the pond. He asks what they are doing and notices their British accents. He tells them they are on private property, and they have to get off the land immediately. Well, one of them tells him, "Oh we're English, and we have English fishing licenses." The sheriff looks at them and tells 'em, "We haven't recognized those since 1776."

-Officer Clayton, Sonoma Police

53

A Piedmont Drive resident called deputies earlier this week and asked them why his wife would not change their kid's diaper.

A resident of Siesta Way said she heard her roommate's car start up Tuesday morning. She said she thought it strange because her roommate was in jail.

> *Whenever I'd go on vacation, I'd come home, and these two friends of mine would have redecorated my yard somehow. Real estate signs: "This house for sale"- all sorts of things. One of them went out of town on vacation, so the two of us decided to redecorate his yard. He had this stone duck on his lawn, so we painted the duck with florescent paint and we positioned a flamingo behind the duck, to appear as it was having its way with the duck, and there were a bunch of flamingos we positioned in line awaiting their turn.*
>
> *-Ray, local*

A Sonoma Valley real estate agent reported to deputies that while she was showing some clients a property, they heard "shots whiz over their head." Three deputies responded to the call, where they found a small firearms range constructed on a neighboring property. Deputies warned the individuals responsible for the shooting, though they could not find any county ordinance or penal code violations prohibiting their activity.

> *I came here 30 years ago and the old timers finally stopped calling me a tourist 5 years ago.*
>
> *-Everett, local*

Residents of San Ramon Road had been under surveillance for suspicion of drug dealing out of the house, according to a detective of the narcotics bureau, who said he expected to find more contraband than that which was confiscated. "When you're dealing with dealers, sometimes they have dope and sometimes not. There's no inventory system like 7-Eleven, with automatic reorder."

SLAM SHOCKS WIFE

A woman told police Thursday that her husband had just shot himself in their Aragon Street bedroom while she was in the shower, and she was afraid to go look. Upon arrival, police discovered that the man had merely slammed the door while on his way to take the laundry out. The husband said he would be taking his wife to Sonoma Valley Hospital for a mild sedative.

She kept calling back on 911, wanting zip code information.
-Officer Reed, Sonoma Police

On Thursday a semi-hysterical Sonoma resident called police to report that an elderly neighbor hadn't been seen for some time, wouldn't answer the phone or door, and had been feeling ill the night before. When police arrived several frantic neighbors were trying to get into the man's house, using ladders and removing window screens. One went in through a small window, ran to the front door, and let police in, without seeing the missing man anywhere. After entering the very warm house, police found the man busy in the bathroom. Officers explained that he was hard of hearing and couldn't stop what he was doing to answer the phone or door.

We once had court at Judge Gravern's house. He was ill and in bed and couldn't make it to the courthouse, **"We once had court at Judge Gravern's house."** *when the courthouse was on the second floor in City Hall. He would give the court order there. Give the sentence and everything from his bed.*
-Officer Thomas, Sonoma Police

Wednesday morning, a woman called police to report a strange car parked on France Street with four persons inside. She said she'd seen the car in the area previously and was worried that the people inside were watching a house. Police said her suspicions were unfounded and the people were really Jehovah Witnesses.

We got a tip that there was some shady stuff going on. It was an illegal bingo set up inside, and they'd locked the doors. Betting on bingo was illegal back then, the betting and the money. We acted on the tip. We start banging on the doors, and nobody was answering. When they knew it was us, everyone took off running out the back, and we let everyone go, **"Everyone took off** *except we talked to* **running out the back."** *a couple of the guys who were running it. We told them not to do it anymore. We could arrest you, but we're not going to do that. And it worked.*

— *Officer Thomas, Sonoma Police*

A San Arroyo Road resident reported at 1 a.m. Sunday that she could feel music vibrations. Police could not find the source of the music or the vibrations.

A person with hands tied behind his back, was being forced into a Volkswagen by two other people Tuesday, according to a Berkeley Street resident who witnessed the abduction. It was later learned by police that the suspicious incident was actually part of a "send off party" for someone going to France.

A First Street West resident said she saw a black man trying to break into cars in a parking lot near her home. Police said it turned out to be a tanned man, cleaning his car.

We had a lady calling us at 911 to come over to change the channel on her T.V.

-Officer Jenkins, Sonoma Police

Doorbell ditchers are working the area of West Spain Street.

It was Jim's first trip out of the house since he had his heart attack. He decided to do some errands and walk through town to a few places. He went by himself and was gone for a couple of hours. Well, before he gets home there is a knock at the door. I answer it and it's officer Thomas. I said, "Hi Frank." He said, "Hi Anne. I just wanted to let you know that Jim did great today. I followed him around to make sure he was all right, but I don't think he saw me. He's on his way home now, so I should go. He did really great." It brought a tear to my eye. When Jim got home I asked him how his walk was and he said, "Great. It was odd, I saw Frank about 3 times today, I don't think he saw me though."

-Anne, local

A Valley woman reported Friday that a man she hired to pick her peaches sat down and ate one when he finished the job.

They backed [the car] up across the street, backed through the garage, straight through the back of the garage and into the swimming pool. Then, I guess they got out of the car, went inside and went to sleep. We got the call and went over there and garage door was closed, must have dropped down when they went through the back wall. Looked normal from the street. Well, we walked around, looked over the fence, and, sure as s%* t, **"The car was in the pool with the hood sticking out."** *the car was in the pool with the hood sticking out. No-*

> *body answered the door and so they must have gone in,*
> *turned off the lights, and went to sleep.*
>
> *-Officer Thomas, Sonoma Police*

Deputies responded to the home of an elderly couple in Glen Ellen when the man claimed his wife threatened to burn their home down "because she hated it and wants to move to Sonoma city limits," the sheriff's log stated.

> *Some woman called me to go into her mom's house and*
> *make sure her mom's electric blanket was on. I asked her,*
> *"Won't I scare her?"* **"It makes you feel good**
> *"Oh no, she sleeps* **because you helped**
> *like a log." She told* **somebody."**
> *me where the key*
> *was. I snuck in the bedroom, saw the electric blanket*
> *was on, snuck out, locked the door and called her. That's*
> *the public service part. It makes you feel good because*
> *you helped somebody. That's what it's all about, taking*
> *care of the community.*
>
> *-Officer Flynn, Sonoma Police*

Police were called to the area of Sonoma Valley Hospital late Saturday on the report of a disturbance. All they could find was a man "walking, practicing karate."

> *If they are really drunk, I always stay out front of the*
> *house and make sure that they get in through the door.*
> *There are great locals who have had a few too many at*
> *the bar, and you want to make sure they are home and*
> *they're safe.*
>
> *-Gordon, cabbie*

A woman reported the sound of running water in front of her house on East Napa Street at 4:51 a.m. on Friday. Police told the woman her sprinklers were on.

It had to be around 4:30 in the morning, and somebody jacked all four tires off my patrol car. Right in front of my house, 70 feet from my bedroom window.

-Officer Hamil, Sonoma Security

Saturday afternoon, a caller reported that he found a rather strange item resembling an expended missile outside his apartment complex on Second Street West.

There was a Bingo game for years in Father Roberts Hall at Saint Francis. There was a fire in the hall one night. We called 911, and all of the services- Sonoma, Boyes Springs-arrived because it was at a school. We ushered everyone out of there as quick as can be. But everyone stayed outside and waited for the firemen to put out the fire. No one left to go home. All of the players were just waiting to get back in there and finish the game. The fire-fighters couldn't work fast enough. And sure as can be, as soon as they were done, all of the players rushed back in to finish **"They just wanted to play more Bingo."** *the game. They didn't care about the smoke… they just wanted to play more Bingo.*

-Alice, local

A citizen said a strange person, "possibly Bigfoot," was spotted walking down Fourth Street East late Tuesday.

Back then so many of the officers lived in the area. There was a rule that you had to live in the city limits to be a police officer. They were married to some of the locals. Their kids went to school together. We did things together because we did live close; we shared neighborhoods.

-Officer Flynn, Sonoma Police

A resident of Seventh Street West called police Sunday, complaining that a man was in her backyard "doing yard work against her requests." The mysterious laborer was gone by the time police arrived.

When my granddaughter was little, this one CHP officer, every once in a while, would pull into my driveway if he saw us outside or saw my car was home. He'd pull into the driveway and turn his outside speaker on and say something. Scared the daylights out of my granddaughter because she couldn't figure out where the voice was coming from.

-Officer Reed, Sonoma Police

CRIME IN PROGRESS TURNS OUT TO BE TV

A Valley resident who was walking past a France Street house heard someone say, "Oh my God" and nothing more, it was reported Wednesday evening. Police went to see what the problem was and learned the subjects were just watching television.

DEPUTIES FIND FIRED-UPON, CATSUPPED DUMMY IN TREE

Sonoma Valley Sheriff's Deputies were summoned to Apple Valley Road to investigate what appeared to be a body dangling from a tree, spotted by a busload of children Wednesday afternoon. Officers, responding to the eastside Sonoma area, found a hanging 5-foot plaster dummy, complete with a shaped face, collarbone and all. The dummy had numerous bullet holes in it, of varying sizes. It also had a heart drawn on it and appeared to be splattered with ketchup. It was taken down and transported to the substation.

I take an older lady over to Petaluma every couple of weeks so she can do her shopping. It'll be on my day off. I figure I'm going over there anyway, and I can help her out.

-Ellen, cabbie

Someone reported a tall man hanging on a street sign at the corner of Este Madera Court and Este Madera Drive Monday.

A manhole cover on Verano Avenue was pried open Wednesday and "half the neighborhood was playing inside," according to sheriff's reports.

> *I have gone into houses and lit furnaces for little old ladies.*
> *-Officer Flynn, Sonoma Police*

MAN TAKES CHAINSAW TO HOUSE
A resident of Hutchinson Avenue reported Tuesday, Oct. 26, that her husband was chopping up their house with a chainsaw. Deputies received the call around 3:30 p.m., but the man had fled by the time they arrived. The woman told deputies that she was having an argument with the man when he fired up his chainsaw and started cutting chunks out of the wall of the home.

> *At one of our reunions, we were told Earl was going to come. I walked up to Earl and said, "How you been?" Which I realized was pretty stupid right away, because he'd just gotten out of prison, where he had been for the last 10 years.*
> *-Sean, local*

Someone set a bag of flaming feces on the porch of a home on Anza road, Thursday night. Police have no suspects in the prank.

MYSTERY LEGS
A female resident of Commonwealth Street told police she returned home at night to find a pair of men's legs sticking out the door of her family's Toyota Tundra pickup parked in the driveway of their home. She said as she arrived, the legs emerged, attached to a white male in his 50s with shaggy gray hair, a yellow Tommy Bahama

shirt, shorts and running shoes. The man ran off down the street. The woman inspected the truck and found nothing missing save a few coins, although there was an iPod still resting in the console.

> *When Julia Clegg was dating Owen, Owen was an Ox Roast volunteer who arose every June Ox Roast (one of the popular events in Sonoma) morning, at 4 a.m., to head down to the Plaza and cook the Ox. In their court-ship days, Julia always accompanied him. After they were married, Owen arose at 4 a.m. and shook Julia and said, "Aren't you coming down to help cook the ox?" Julia turned over and pulled up the blankets and said, "Why should I? I got what I was after."*
>
> *-Ray, local*

SHALL WE REDECORATE?

Apparently there is a Sonoma way to do an extreme makeover. My initials, for instance, are still in the cement near the church on Patten Street; many other locals have found extremely creative ways to make their mark in Sonoma.

A resident of Chase Street, told an officer Sunday morning that her new Honda Civic had been "bombed" by Oreo Hydrox cookies (but no milk).

A Jackson Street resident called police on Saturday at midnight to report that a neighbor was pouring gasoline on her lawn to spell out an obscenity. An extra patrol of the neighborhood was made.

> *We t.p.'d her car on a really cold night, late. She was over at somebody's house, and we saw her car. So we layered the toilet paper over the windshield, knowing after a couple of hours it would be frozen. Her dad was pissed, because he knew it was us, and he had to go over and get her because she couldn't drive the car home.*
>
> *-Ron, local*

A Fifth Street West resident reported to police that a dead skunk was placed in his car sometime during the night Saturday. The car owner believed the stinky deed may have been performed by a neighbor who is being evicted. Strangely enough, the victim also blames the neighbor for his drunken driving arrest the week before.

> *My brother and I had to spend 3 hours together laying in a bed of ivy one Halloween, hiding from the cops. We were having fun, a group of us, and a new kid decided to grab a pumpkin and toss it through someone's bay window. We scattered. Police showed up, and we were stuck in the ivy for a long time, hiding. I never forgave that kid for ruining our night.*
>
> *-Sam, local*

UNKNOWN ARTIST SPRAY-PAINTS CAR
A woman who was supposed to be watching over her neighbor's house on Bedrock Avenue reported that sometime on Friday, Jan. 8, someone spray-painted the neighbor's entire car black. The woman said that when she last saw the car, it was blue, but when she checked it that evening, it was black, and the rims had been spray-painted green.

> *Someone had put a big, old, gray, clay appendage on the man in the bear flag monument statue. And there were all these Girl Scouts or Brownies, all of them 9-10-11 years of age, and they are there giggling and taking pictures of it while Jim Dobson had to go up and take it off. He didn't speak to us for a few days.*
>
> *-Al, Sonoma Parks Employee*

TOO MUCH TP

The estate manager of a vacant residence on Manhattan Avenue reported that someone had gotten into an unlocked bathroom by the swimming pool, removed a number of rolls of toilet paper, and toilet papered the roof and the pool area.

VANDALS TEAR THOUGH EASTSIDE SONOMA

Vandals were running rampant on the east side of town last weekend as a number of residents complained about uprooted flowers, turned-on water hoses and smashed mailboxes. The telephones at the Sonoma Police Department rang off the hook Saturday morning as victims of the vandalism called to report their findings. Three tiles were torn off a home on Casey Avenue Friday night, according to a resident who also complained about destroyed plants and the missing cover to a cable television box.

> *Every once in a while, a new guy will come into town and hang out in the rose garden area, get all drunk and tear it up, not respect it like the other regulars do, but those guys get put in their place pretty quickly by the regulars. Don't mess it up for us!*
>
> *-Roy, Sonoma Parks Employee*

Someone smashed some benches in the Plaza and used them for firewood, it was reported Monday. Police said they will be on the lookout for such activity.

Crayon graffiti was discovered on a bench in the Sonoma Plaza rose garden. The designs, scrawled in red, orange, yellow, blue, purple and white, included a sun, a snail, and an unknown symbol.

Pumpkin throwers were on the loose on Clyborn Street Thursday. One of the smarter ones was bragging about it later at a nearby gas station. Now, police know who he is.

I came into work at the golf course, and it was a mess.
There were golf carts everywhere: in creeks, in trees, and
in the ditches. It was a disaster. We had to get a tractor
and pull them out of all these places.

-Michael, local

A truck tractor parked on Nuns Canyon Road may have been torched by an arsonist. A heavy-set woman "wearing Levi's that were too small for her" was last seen near the vehicle. The case is being investigated.

HEARTFELT MESSAGE LEADS TO ARREST

A man who may have gotten swept up in the sentiment of Valentine's Day was arrested on suspicion of vandalism this week after he admitted to painting two Broadway billboards with hearts. Police say Chris Patrick Quinn, 44, was probably drunk when he called them at 4:36 a.m. Friday and said he fell off a nearby billboard and had lost his glasses. Quinn told officers he spray-painted the billboards to publicly thank his landlords for allowing him to stay on their property. Quinn will face charges of public drunkenness and vandalism. His glasses were found beneath one of the billboards, police say.

VANDALS STRIKE LITTLE CITY HALL

Little City Hall was struck by vandals Sunday night, causing $500 in damage and lost property. Little City Hall, part of the Club House Family Fun Center's miniature golf course in Maxwell Village, is a scale replica of Sonoma City Hall. The model was broken into sometime before Monday morning. Vandals entered through the automatic door, which allows golfer's shots to reach their destination. In doing so, they broke the door. Once inside, they cut wires for lights and the door, ripped out a light socket, broke plexiglass windows and stole 75 light bulbs.

PUMPKIN SMASHES MAR HALLOWEEN

Criminal impulses were relatively restrained over the witching weekend, but that didn't stop a few vandals from performing some Halloween-season tricks. At about 9:45 p.m. on Friday, Oct. 24, someone tossed an egg at the windshield of a Ford Ranger pick-up truck. Police speculate that the egg may have come from a hen on steroids, or perhaps on a special high-calcium diet, because the egg produced a slight crack in the windshield, suggesting a rather dense shell.

> *I did everything these kids did and worse, in this town.*
> *If they did something stupid, I'd say, "First one is on me,*
> *I'll cut you some slack. But the second one is on you."*
> *-Officer Thomas, Sonoma Police*

The "bumper car" vandals struck again at Sonoma National Golf Course, July 2nd, according to a report filed by Walter McCracken, Superintendent of Grounds at the golf course on Arnold Drive. The culprits broke through a wall of the shed housing the electric carts and rode around the course on them, damaging several carts in the process. Damage was estimated at $1,500. The vandalism occurred between midnight and 4 a.m.

On Friday, a man reported that during the night someone wrapped his car in tissue and then squirted **"Someone wrapped his car in tissue."** ketchup on it. He did not know what brand of TP it was, but said the ketchup smelled like Heinz.

Someone opened the racks of the Index-Tribune newspaper early Friday morning and inserted a sheet of paper with a derogatory message about a valley businessman into the papers.

An incorrectly spelled vulgarity was scrawled on a rain gutter at the Sonoma Community School on First Street West.

A man who lives on Vassell Avenue reported that someone had thrown a rock through the windshield of his car. The rock had a note attached to it, asking the man if he was happy with his new girlfriend. This led the man to conclude that his ex-girlfriend was responsible for the vandalism. He declined to press charges.

> *Someone did the "greased pigs trick" in the big building at the high school. Apparently, someone had taken the pigs from FFA and covered them in grease and released them in the hallways. I don't know who did it, but the janitors were going to have a hell of a time getting ahold of them.*
>
> *-Russell, local*

After hearing reports of a possible break-in at the Simon Levi Tasting Room on Highway 12 in Kenwood late Tuesday, local sheriff's deputies arrived to find the alleged burglar simply sitting on the steps to the entrance. Will Chapman, 47, of Santa Rosa is alleged to have activated a silent alarm in his efforts to enter the building. Within three or four minutes, deputies from the local Valley Substation arrived to find Chapman sitting near a broken window and unlatched the door. The deputy on the scene said three football-sized rocks had been thrown into the window. The deputy reported the suspect saying, "I guess you'll have to arrest me, I broke in. I was just thinking about buying the place," when he shined his flashlight into the suspect's eyes.

Another 16-year-old boy was arrested Monday for vandalism involving spray paint on walls at Sonoma Marketplace. The lad left incriminating

"The lad had left incriminating evidence written on the walls-his name."

evidence written on the walls—his name. Clever police work followed to nab the suspect. Reports are that two others who left similar calling cards will be picked up this week.

In what could be an ominous sign, three trash barrels were tagged in 18000 block of Highland Boulevard. The barrels were tagged with mathematical signs, so officers are on the lookout for a roving pack of nerds.

> *We carried this guy's VW bug from the parking lot to the center octagon at the high school. Six of us picked it up and moved it.*
>
> -*Russell, local*

Someone smeared peanut butter on the doors, door handles and door locks of the Sonoma Valley Library on West Napa Street.

An unknown subject threw auto parts through a window of an auto parts store on Napa Street. The suspect was believed to be a distraught customer and escaped on a bicycle.

A 28-year-old Sonoma woman was spotted by police writing graffiti on the Depot Park gazebo while moderately intoxicated and on probation for prior acts of vandalism. Had she not been caught in the act, the woman might nevertheless have been arrested, because part of what she wrote on the gazebo was her full name.

THE PLAZA

Beautiful? Yes! Historic? Absolutely! Characters welcomed? WITHOUT A DOUBT! I learned how to juggle from a clown in the Pickle Family Circus who used to practice in the Plaza. Years ago, an old local used to drink tall boys of Hamm's beer in the Plaza, and everyone would yell "Hi!" to him out their car windows. One of the best harmonica players I've ever heard was in charge of keeping the Plaza looking great for 37 years.

Officers found a chandelier flying from the flagpole in front of city hall Friday.

> *The Plaza is geographically ideally structured so there is a center to it. It's centered to the square and holy s%*t... you can drink there... legally! Those are elements that conspire to create events, incidents, and behavior patterns.*
>
> *-Jim, local*

PLAZA 'FREQUENT FLIERS' ATTRACT DEPUTIES' ATTENTION

Police call them "frequent flyers" because of the regularity of their visits to the Plaza - and county jail. They are a small but dependable band of citizens who share a fondness for alcohol, marijuana - and congregating near the rose garden. Invariably their presence attracts the attention of police.

Teens were swinging from the flagpole into the duck pond in the Plaza late Saturday.

> *I was in high school, and I went on a diet. We lived a few blocks off the square. I walked down to the square and went to Food City and bought a Butterfinger candy bar. I walked into the park, sat down on a bench and ate it. When I got home, my mom asked me what I was doing in the park eating a Butterfinger. I was shocked. I asked her how she could have known that so quickly. She told me that Charlie, the police officer, had called. He apparently knew I was supposed to be on a diet and saw me in the park eating the candy bar and called my mom to tell her I was cheating. It's a pretty small town.*
>
> *-Tina, local*

A business on the Sonoma Plaza called police Thursday to report that a man was lying on the ground in front of their store. When police arrived, the man said he was waiting for a friend. He was instructed to wait in the park.

> *He was pretty drunk and left the Town Square Bar. On his way out, he turned* **"Don't worry! I have a cab."** *around and yelled, "Don't worry! I have a cab." He walked right out the front door, opened the back door of the car and got in. Only problem was it was a Sonoma*

Police car, not a cab. They serve pretty good drinks at The Town Square Bar.

-Mollie, local

While on call in the Plaza, officers ran into a man carrying a large amount of frozen meat. The man was taken into custody by police and later released without charges.

There was this bookie in town. Nice guy, but he liked to drink a lot. He told me this story: One day he was drunk and crossing the street in the middle of the day, from the Cheese Factory to the park. He apparently stumbled in the crosswalk, so the cops stopped him and busted him for being drunk in public. They took him down to the station and booked him. They made him empty out his pockets and he's got a roll of 100's and 20's on him. Mind you, they didn't know he was the town bookie. Well, one of the cops starts to freak out, and he turns to the other cop saying, "Oh my god, you know what we got here? You know what we got here?!!" The other cop looks at him baffled, trying to put it together, and the cop who's freaking out says, "Looks like we got a pimp in town!"

-Ash, local

A 28-year-old man was found climbing City Hall Saturday. He told police he wasn't climbing it for any particular reason, only that it was there.

One day my friends talked me into driving around the Plaza backwards in my car. I did two laps in reverse and didn't get caught.

-Henry, local

Kids in a car were shooting tourists with a water gun at the Plaza on Monday afternoon. The cops admonished the sharp shooters and told their parents.

There were shots fired one night at the Cheese Factory. The fire department and us (police) arrived. Somebody was inside, but we didn't know who. The Chief of Police was on the roof of the Cheese Factory when he attempted to throw a canister of tear gas through the window in order for flush the suspects out. But the canister bounced off the edge of the window and dropped down on all of us waiting on the sidewalk in front. That was a mess. Everybody's eyes were tearing up and they were coughing. He finally got one into the window. We **"There were shots fired one night at the Cheese Factory."** *eventually got inside and found these two guys upstairs, drunk as a skunk. One worked there and the other was a local. They apparently just got really drunk and started goofing around and shooting the gun. We'd see the two guys a couple of months later, wave to them and they would wave back.*

-Officer Thomas, Sonoma Police

MAN GETS SLAPPED 3 TIMES BY TEEN

On Thursday, a 23-year-old man reported that he was slapped in the face three times by an 18-year-old girl in the Plaza Rose Garden. The man said he overheard the woman making disparaging remarks about him and when he confronted her about it, she slapped him. He asked her again why she was saying such things, and she slapped him a second time. He then asked her why she continued to slap him, and she responded by slapping him a third time. The man walked away to find a police officer before his assailant could slap him a fourth time.

We knew the cops called us The Plaza Rats, but we had our own name: the Park Cronies (the old friends).

-Jimmy, local

A 33-year-old man and his fiancée were walking down First Street West, returning to his father's house, when he laughed at something his fiancée said. Two young men on the opposite sidewalk, apparently thinking he was laughing a them, began shouting insults. The man said he wasn't addressing them and continued to his father's home where shortly afterward he heard the sound of something striking the house. He went outside, where the two young men attacked him. He fought back and began **"Is that 'Stupid'?"** chasing them back up First Street West to the Plaza where, according to police, they entered a restaurant. Police had been called and one officer entered the back of the establishment while the other went in the front. Each officer corralled a suspect trying to exit. The first suspect, 21, was asked to identify his alleged accomplice and said he knew him only as "Stupid." When police pointed to the second suspect, now sitting in a patrol car, and asked, "Is that 'Stupid'?" the man said, "Oh, do whatever you have to do." The 22-year-old sitting in the patrol car appeared to be highly intoxicated and visibly emotional, police said. Both Sonoma men were charged with battery and booked into the county jail.

Probably 70% percent of the establishments on the Plaza serve alcohol.

-Jim, local

NO PLACE TO PEE
In a doorway next to a popular Plaza saloon, police on foot patrol spotted a man with his back to the sidewalk and a stream of fluid flowing past his feet. The officers interrupted his reverie with a question, to wit: Why don't you just pee in the tavern? The man explained that he couldn't because he wasn't 21 and couldn't go inside.

We filled the fountain up with detergent in the Plaza and sat there in the car waiting for the fountain to go on. It was around 5 a.m. We real- ized we were **"We filled the water fountain up with detergent."** *the only ones parked on the square in front of the fountain. As soon as the bubbles would overflow and come down the sidewalk toward a car with 5 kids in it, it would lead to us getting busted. Not many people hanging out at that time. So we took off pretty fast.*

-Russell, local

A LICENSE TO WET YOUR LIPS

A California driver's license is approximately 2-inches by 3.5 inches in size and flat as a ... well, it's really flat. A Chapstick is about 2-inches long, half-an-inch wide and utterly round. These spatial distinctions would not concern the average citizen, but then the average citizen would not be passed out on a Plaza park bench at 1:54 in the morning. That's the time Sonoma police discovered a 26-year-old San Francisco man on Friday, Aug. 5, bench surfing and dead to the world. It took an officer repeated attempts to wake the wastrel from a sleep enhanced, all evidence indicated, by generous, if not extravagant, amounts of alcohol. Finally roused to something approaching consciousness, the recumbent visitor mumbled something unintelligible to an officer who in turn asked him for some form of identification. The man fumbled through his pockets searching for ID and finally handed it to the officer. It was, of course, a tube of Chapstick, which has never, to Google's knowledge, been successfully employed as a legal license to drive.

The bench jockey was determined to be in a condition in which he might be a danger to himself or others and for which Chapstick would be no help. He was therefore charged with public intoxication and booked into the county jail.

STUPID IS...

Most people would think that you have a crime in mind, you plan it and you execute it. Like on T.V. or in Films. But ask any cop and they'll tell you that's far from the truth. Sometimes the crime is stupid, sometimes the criminal.

Four college kids chowed down at the Vineyards Inn Friday night and then took off without paying for their meal. One not-so-alert boy made the mistake of giving a waitress his name and phone number. Deputies found the group camping in Sugarloaf Park and gave them a day to pay their $35.35 (plus tip) tab.

> *My sister's ex and his buddy lived across the street from the Fruit Basket. They decided to steal watermelons one night and grabbed more than they could carry. The police followed the trail of broken watermelons to their front door and arrested them.*
>
> *-Michelle, local*

UP A TREE WITH LIMITED OPTIONS
Deputies were sent to a residence on Verdugo Road after a resident reported that someone was inside her house. By the time deputies arrived, the intruder had fled the residence. Deputies headed to a

nearby home where they had prior contact with some of the residents. On their way, they saw a man who matched the description of the trespasser. The man ran from the deputies and climbed a tree, a strategy that seldom works for domestic cats, bears or fleeing intruders, there being limited further options. According to the police report, when he inevitably jumped from the tree, the man fought with deputies before they were able to subdue him.

I think his name was Aaron Lawler. He told everyone he was going to break a two-by-four over his head in the park. He was like 17 years old. He had long hair. So, everybody went to the park after school and gathered around. He walked with his group of friends and had a two-by-four over his **"He told everyone he was going to break a two-by-four over his head."** *shoulder. Everyone gasped when he actually showed up. We gathered in a circle around him. It was near the Bear Flag statue. He lifted up the piece of wood and slammed it down on his head. It didn't break. He tried it three times and it still didn't break. Everyone went home disappointed, he went home with a headache and bruised ego.*

-Andrew, local

BRILLIANT POLICE WORK NABS MAPLE TREE THIEF

Sometimes the investigative acumen demonstrated by officers of the law is singularly impressive. Consider the case of the missing maple tree, stolen out of the ground from a site near the Jolly Washer car wash on Sonoma Highway on the night of May 17. When police arrived at the scene of the crime at 9:40 the next morning, they found an empty hole in the ground and no sign of the tree. There was, however, a trail of dirt and mud leading away from the hole and police cleverly deduced that the dirt trail was likely connected to the tree theft. They then followed the trail down Ramon Street, where it led to the backyard of a residence.

Further investigation revealed a 6-foot, red leaf maple, lying on the ground with its root ball largely destroyed. Police knocked on the door of the home and eventually a man answered while standing behind the closed screen door. Asked what the tree was doing in his yard, the man exclaimed, "Where did that come from? I've never seen that before!" Police told the man to come outside so they could question him further, so he stepped through the door wearing only a T-shirt and underpants. Police then suggested the man put some proper pants on, so he went back into the home and emerged moments later in a pair of blue jeans. Police could not help noticing that the pants were heavily coated with dirt and dried mud. When officers pointed out the obvious evidence - the dirt trail leading from the crime scene, the tree in the backyard, the muddy pants - the suspect shook his head back and forth dejectedly and finally admitted, "Yeah, I took the tree. I was drunk last night."

Some punks, they forget they ran on you [without paying], but I remember. It's a small town. This one guy, two months after he ran on me, calls for a pick-up. I get there, and he's got his girlfriend with him and they are going on a date. I said to him, "Hey you remember me?" He's like, "Oh man, yeah, that was all a mistake... That was all a mistake." I told him, "Ok, why don't you slip a twenty through the window and we'll consider it a mistake." He slipped the twenty through, "Okay, sir." "Yes, sir."

-Gordon, cabbie

A developer of a condominium complex on Agua Caliente road discovered that a large sign advertising the development had been removed from his property on May 14. A short distance away he discovered that the sign had been made into two planter boxes by a neighbor resident who said he thought the sign had been abandoned. The planter box maker agreed to pay the victim for the sign.

Sometimes when I'm dispatching, I get a call from some-one who wants a cab, but they don't know where they are. That makes it a little difficult to pick them up.

-Red, cabbie

DUDE, WHERE'S MY CAR? NO, REALLY!

When Sonoma police received a report about a suspicious vehicle they discovered a red 2000 Pontiac Grand Prix, unlocked, with the key in the ignition and the motor still running. It was about 11:30 p.m., but after the officer turned off the motor, a quick check of the registration revealed the owner was a Santa Rosa woman who happened to be home and awake when police called to ask if she knew where her car was. "It should be outside on the street," she said. Asked to go look, she came back to the phone to report the car was gone. The absence of the car did not come as a complete surprise when the owner explained that her key had become stuck in the ignition some time ago, and when she couldn't get it out she began draping a T-shirt over the steering column and locking all the doors while leaving a rear window rolled down just far enough for her to reach in and unlock the car. Her meager security measures had obviously failed, but the good news was that the car was undamaged and the investigating police officer reported no difficulty extracting the key. And while nothing was missing from the car, there were several new objects inside it that did not belong to the owner, including a wood-handled knife with the name "Isaac" carved into it, a cell phone, a bottle of fruit flavored vodka and some cosmetology products.

Two cops went to check an open door on a roof at night. They went up on the rooftop, and the door shut behind them. It was locked. So the only two cops on duty for 2-½ square miles are locked on a roof. They were think-ing about shooting the lock. They eventually got in touch with a secretary to come to work early, swing by and open the door for them.

-Phillip, local

Deputies spotted a man drinking a beer on a corner and stopped to talk to him. They asked the 25-year-old man his name, but suspected he wasn't telling the truth when the one he gave differed from the one hanging around his neck by a gold necklace.

This was at a restaurant on the Plaza. One customer was a total snob. He was one of those tourists trying to impress his girl and talking down to the staff. He was stupid because he asked for a bottle of the "Kor-cauge." Only after a few minutes of trying to figure out what bottle he wanted **"He asked for a bottle of the Kor-cauge."** *did I realize he thought we had a bottle on the list for $15. It was the "corkage" fee. It felt good to tell him what that actually was. Idiot.*

-Mollie, local

A subject was cited and released for public intoxication in front of the police department.

A guy carved his name in the new cement in the area on Highway 12 Tuesday. It wasn't hard to figure out who did it and the culprit was given a bucket and water and ordered to smooth over his artwork.

Two men inquiring about a recently-arrested buddy Saturday morning were caught snooping around the police station. One, John Moles was arrested for allegedly stealing a flashlight out of a patrol car.

I saw these two kids come into the store, and one is wearing a backpack with the zipper open. So I follow them around the store, and sure enough I see one kid stuffing things in the backpack. No tact. I told them, "Look, you are not good at this! Stop it." Some kids are pretty stupid.

-Officer Hamil, Sonoma Security

What do you do if you're underage, it's Friday night, and you want to party? If you're a couple of impulsive and criminally inept high school students, you walk into a convenience store on Arnold Drive and steal two 12-packs of beer while your admiring girlfriends wait outside and a surveillance camera films the entire escapade. It did not take sheriff's deputies long to review the surveillance tape and identify the students, who were attending Sonoma Valley High School.

> *He decided to run on the fare after we got to where we were going. I guess he forgot that he called for the cab with his* **"I think that qualified for a Darwin Award."** *own cell phone number. Wasn't hard to track him down. I think that qualified for a Darwin award.*
>
> *-Gordon, cabbie*

Deputies contacted a man at the intersection of Highway 12 and Siesta Way and arrested him for giving a false name to a peace officer, as well as for an outstanding warrant. When asked for his name, the man reportedly told deputies he was Bob Dylan.

OH THOSE KIDS

G rowing up in Sonoma was great. We were bored sometimes and that led us to do some pretty stupid and
creative things. Pluming cars, Doorbell ditching, Mailbox
baseball and giving direction to tourists that the Mission
was 12 miles west on Highway 12 when it was actually 2
blocks away.

Several teenagers were caught at 1:24 a.m. Sunday after police responded to a call that they had broken into the pool area at Moon
Valley Mobile Home Park. The boys fled when police arrived, leaving behind their clothes, car keys, and wallets. They were caught a
few blocks away. The officer who caught them said in his report,
"They were easy to spot. They were the only ones with wet Fruit of
the Looms."

*We had a family Suburban with tinted windows. It was
my dad's. We would drive down to the Plaza on a busy
Saturday. I would drive and my buddies would be in the
back. Tourists everywhere. We'd drive around, and when
the moment was right, I'd stop the car at the busiest* **We called it "Suburban
B.A.-ing."** *corner, slam on the horn and pull the windows down.*

I had all the controls right there. All these people would look over at the car and all they would see is a couple of bare asses staring at them. Then we would take off, laughing like crazy. We pissed a few people off. We called it "Suburban B.A.-ing."

-Justin, local

A clerk at the 7-Eleven store on West Napa Street told police that two teen-age boys just purchased a carton of eggs and were laughing as they left the store Wednesday. They left in a green pickup.

The first time I met my girlfriend's mom, I was in a jail cell with her daughter. She had to come pick her daughter and me up at the jail because we had been caught partying up in the hills.

-Seth, local

Someone reported a man standing next to a white car with a bouquet of flowers and a rifle on Sunday. The man turned out to be a juvenile, the weapon a pellet gun. Police spotted him later and checked out the weapon.

We were drinking up in the hills, and then we hear some noises and we see flashlights. It's the cops. So we scattered. I was wearing Birkenstocks and was only able to grab one of them, the other I left on the blanket. And we can hear them going through our stuff. Blanket, beers, bottles. Yelling to us to come out of the bushes. But that wasn't going to happen. No one was moving and they weren't about to come searching in the bushes. So, sure **"They left everything else, except my Birkenstock."** *enough, after a while the cops finally leave. When we get back to the blanket, I saw they had taken my Birken-*

stock. Dammit. That was pretty smart, because they knew I couldn't go far. They left everything else, except my Birkenstock. Booze bottles, everything. By the time we got down the hill, they were waiting at my car. They had already run the plates and knew it was mine.

-Seth, local

I was bustin' up a party, telling the kids to get out of here, get going, and I hear, "Hi Daddy!" It was my daughter. I rolled my eyes, told her to get home too.

-Officer Thomas, Sonoma Police

The manager at a pizza parlor in the Sonoma Marketplace reported that five kids were "mooning" his restaurant just after midnight yesterday.

We were making wine coolers long before Bartles and James showed up. We hated the taste of wine when we were in high school, so we'd mix it up with a 2-liter of 7up.

-Andy, local

Police received a report that kids in a Valley Mart Laundromat were causing a disturbance Friday afternoon. When they got there, they found youngsters "quietly folding laundry." They were warned anyway.

Rob's mom would make a birthday cake and put coins in the cake. Quarters. Nickles. Dimes. I chipped my tooth at his birthday party eating that cake, and the worst part is that I chipped it on a nickel. His mom was screaming with excitement, "You got the nickel! You got the nickel!" I was so mad. I chipped my tooth on a lousy nickel.

-Seth, local

The parents of a 19-year-old man reported him missing Tuesday. The man had gone to a reggae festival over the weekend in Mendocino County with two friends named "Poppie" and "Freebie," but had not returned home. The man turned up a couple of days later, a week after leaving.

> *The Swarm of Thornes was a good make-out spot. It was directly behind the buildings on the east side of the Plaza where Food City and Arcados were located. They were these big blackberry bushes on the edge of a field that had these little open spots in the middle of the bushes where you could hang out and not be seen.*
>
> *-Seth, local*

Six kids were "mooning" passing motorists late Tuesday in the area of Highway 12 and the bike path.

> *We would call Teen Safe Ride, and Jerry would be praying, "Please don't be my dad! Please don't be my dad!" And sure enough his dad's van would pull up because his dad was the volunteer adult driver that night. Busted.*
>
> *-Jeremy, local*

Callers reported several teens trying to climb the face of City Hall Sunday. They were admonished and told to knock it off.

> *There was a girl from a prominent winery family and she was driving up the hill with some friends and a bunch of beer. I pulled them over on Norrbom Road and made them dump it all out. I told them to, "Get your butts home, get outta here." And this girl turns around and says, "Officer Thomas, if you tell my dad, will you tell him it was wine?"*

"If you tell my dad, will you tell him it was wine?"

> *-Officer Thomas, Sonoma Police*

TEENS IRATE ABOUT BOOZE BUST

Three juveniles on their way to a football game were arrested at 8 p.m., Friday, for possession of alcohol in Depot Park, on First Street West. As they were being arrested, officers reported that the three teens were rude and complained bitterly about the unjust nature of the alcohol laws in the United States, especially when compared to those in Europe and Mexico.

> *We organized those punk shows in the community center. The parents would come down to the show because they knew they could find their kid there. If they hadn't seen the kid in 2 days, they knew they would be at the show.*
>
> *-Anderson, local*

The clerk at the Vineyard Market on Highway 12 reported that a teenager tried to use a phony $20 bill to buy a lighter. The clerk took the bill and told the kid to get lost, at which point the youth "looked surprised and was about to cry."

> *It would be 10 o'clock at night and we'd be bored at the gas station near Safeway. Billy would spray carburetor starter fluid on the soles of his shoes* **"Light them on fire while he ran across the intersection."** *and light them on fire while he ran across the intersection, flailing his arms and yelling. People would slam on their brakes. It was hilarious.*
>
> *-Jeremy, local*

> *This is going way back. I'd steal my dad's car while the folks were watching a movie at Sebastiani Theatre. We'd drive around, smacking mailboxes. Then I'd drive backward, in reverse, because the old cars would reverse the odometer, and try to park it in the same spot. I never told [my dad] that.*
>
> *-Ted, local*

Employees at Albertsons called police Tuesday night to alert them to a group of teens who were buying a large quantity of eggs. Officers talked to the kids who agreed maybe they didn't need the eggs after all and arranged for the eggs to be returned to the store for cash.

I had a fake ID, but it wasn't that good. My brother gave me the idea to grab some beer and some baby food and some diapers and that would convince the market clerk that I was old enough. I was surprised how many times that worked. And one of my buddies, who smoked a lot of weed, always ate the baby food by the end of the night.
-Andrew, local

I was good to the kids, and the kids were good to me.
-Officer Thomas, Sonoma Police

THE FORBIDDEN WEED

It was kind of like the scene in E.T. where they all ride their bikes through the neighborhood and E.T. is in the basket on one of the bikes. Except we didn't have E.T., we had two big Glad garbage bags full of weed. It was the beginning of summer, I was 15 at the time and there were 5 of us. We rode our BMX bikes across town to a house where we knew they grew weed. One of us was a lookout on the main drag, another was the lookout at the corner of the street and the third was in front of the house. Two of us went over the back fence, pulled up a few 5 foot plants, and stuffed them in the bags. And off we rode back across town with the bags full. We ended up going to summer school in the morning, smoking weed and swimming every afternoon until my buddy's mom came home early from work and busted us. And that was the end of the party. The first time I got super high, my buddy asked me, "Do you know what this is?" I said, "No." and he said "This is the best weed out there, this is the Sonoma Coma." Some pretty funny stuff happens when you're high, even in the Police reports.

TOKERS TAKE FLIGHT

Deputies were sent to El Verano Elementary School on the report that some juveniles were smoking marijuana. When deputies arrived, they surreptitiously counted about 15 individuals and decided to attempt a pincer move, with one deputy approaching from the front and the other from the rear, in case some of the tokers took flight.

> *Sometimes the school bus would be filled with pot smoke. The bus driver would get so mad. He'd stop the bus and he could never find the joint, because we would either toss it out the window or hide it really well.*
>
> *-Seth, local*

A marijuana grower was operating out of a Boyes Hot Springs apartment complex, according to an anonymous caller who telephoned deputies about 10:30 p.m. Saturday night. Deputies went to the complex and found a single marijuana plant about 18 inches high planted near the communal garbage cans. Because the marijuana plant was in a relatively public area, deputies couldn't tell who owned it. They said they confiscated the plant and left their business card in case the pot grower "desired to claim the plant at a later date." The plant was taken for destruction, they said.

> *This girl was going to have a party, a slumber party, at her house, and we were mad that we weren't invited. Well, since we weren't invited we printed up fliers that said, "PARTY! ALL NIGHT, 8 O'CLOCK 'TIL YOUR MOMMY WANTS YOU HOME! SIX POUNDS OF OPIUM DIPPED BUD. 5 KEGS OF ASSORTED BEER! BE THERE* **"Six pounds of opium dipped bud."** *OR BE SOBER!" And we posted them all around. Well, they had so many people show up, hanging out on the front lawn, ringing the doorbell all night long.*
>
> *-Russell, local*

A practical joker placed a six-foot tall marijuana plant in front of Safeway among the store's other garden products early Wednesday morning. One

"A six-foot tall marijuana plant in front of Safeway."

of the store's assistant managers called police and said the plant "is not one of our regularly stocked items."

It was 1:33 a.m. on Saturday, June 5, when a young man showed up at the Sonoma Safeway store sweating profusely and exhibiting behavior more commonly seen in a younger, more pediatric environment, or perhaps at a rave. Police were called and encountered the 19-year-old Sonoma man inside the store, still sweating and still sucking on a pacifier. It was the kind of device that provides oral satisfaction and emotional comfort for kids from zero to maybe 3 years of age or, occasionally, somewhat older individuals under the influence of a psychoactive stimulant. Details of the police interrogation are limited but the

"Still sweating and still sucking on a pacifier."

available report suggests the young man was carrying an open container of alcohol inside the store, that he had less than a gram of marijuana on his person and that he was reasonably intoxicated. Whether he entered the store with the alcohol or obtained it on site was unclear. He was cited for consumption of alcohol by a minor and possession of less than an ounce of marijuana and released. Police did not report what became of the pacifier.

A man walked into the Record Depot at 500 W. Napa Street Tuesday and proceeded to put down three lines of cocaine on the counter. He said the stuff was a "sample," according to the police report and set his "business card" next to the lines. His card contained his name and phone number. Store employees called Sonoma Police, who tested the substance, then entered the name and number into their computer banks as a suspected user. No further action was taken.

It is amazing the stupid things people do when they are in cabs. They get in there, and they'd actually do drug deals in my car.

-Gordon, cabbie

A 24-year-old man was arrested for smoking marijuana in the Plaza Park. When asked if the man was smoking the drug for medicinal purposes, the man said he was not, but did note that he had a hyperactive thyroid.

TOKING IN THE ROSES

A Sonoma police officer spotted a familiar figure in the Plaza rose garden sucking furtively on an odd-shaped cigarette and sharing it with a friend. The officer called the 61-year-old toker over for questioning. The owner of the joint was cited for furnishing less than an ounce of marijuana.

"Safest place to smoke pot in the plaza is the rose garden. You can see them coming."

-Jerry, local

MAN STOPPED FOR EARMUFF VIOLATION

A bicyclist was arrested for possession of marijuana for sale last Sunday afternoon after an officer pulled him over in the 100 block of First Street West for wearing headphones while operating a bicycle. It turned out that the 43-year-old Santa Rosa man was not wearing headphones, but earmuffs. The cyclist, Alex Muto, disputed the legality of the officer's stop, and told him so numerous times. The officer had the man sit on the ground, and proceeded to search the man's backpack. Therein the officer found numerous packages of marijuana for sale.

Don't ride a bike at night without a light on it. If you do, the likelihood that you're high is pretty good.

-Alex, local

Police found that a man selling glasses of store-bought wine from a cooler during the Sonoma Valley Vintage Festival in Sonoma Plaza did not have a permit for same. However, he did have a plastic bag containing a stone pipe, a small quantity of marijuana, and someone else's library card.

ROOMIES BICKER OVER BONG

Police responded to a loud quarrel at an apartment on Falk Street, where they found two male roommates arguing over who took the other's shoes, coins and bong. No arrests were made or injuries reported.

MAN REPORTS THEFT OF POT

A Glen Ellen resident called Sonoma County Sheriff's deputies Sunday evening to report the theft of a "large amount" of marijuana from his home. The 39-year old man assured deputies that the weed was not his. He also said he wanted extra patrol for the area around his Wagner Drive house. A former tenant, whom he suspects of stealing the weed, is calling, saying "nasty and threatening remarks," he told officers. He said he believes the ex-tenant sold the missing marijuana.

"Where you going?" "Oh. I left a CD at a friend's house." So this person is spending $45 on a round-trip cab ride to Glen Ellen to pick up a CD... hmmm. I don't think they're grabbing a CD.

-Gordon, cabbie

BAREFOOT WITH ECSTASY

Citizens who encountered a shoeless man carrying flowers and asking people for help, contacted Sonoma police and a squad car arrived moments later to find the man at the corner of West Napa Street and Second Street West. As the car approached, the man suddenly began sprinting hard directly toward it, forcing the officer at the wheel to accelerate around the corner to avoid a collision. The barefoot vagabond thereupon reclined in the street and, as the officer approached, rolled over onto his back and began doing sit-ups. Asked if he had been drinking, the man confided he had consumed "some shots (of alcohol) and some ecstasy." He also explained that he had no idea where his shoes were, and that he had been at a party, but he didn't know where.

He was charged with public intoxication and a probation violation and spent the rest of New Year's Eve at the county jail.

> *They would just pull their trucks up to the front of the store late at night and load flowers. I would ask, "What the hell are you doing?" "Oh, I'm going to come back tomorrow and pay you." Yeah, right. I can't believe that some guy is stealing flowers to resell, to support his drug habit.*
>
> *-Dan, store security*

SMOKE-FILLED CAR WASN'T ON FIRE

While responding to a loud party on Racine Avenue shortly after 10 p.m. on Saturday, May 2, a deputy walked by a vehicle that he couldn't see into because smoke

"After catching a whiff of the smoke-filled car, decided the pungent odor was herbal."

had filled the car. The deputy at first thought the car was on fire, but after catching a whiff of the smoke-filled car, decided the pungent odor was herbal. After getting the four occupants out of the car, the deputy discovered about 14 grams of marijuana and a number of open beers.

GOT A 420, DUDE?

Four skateboarders at the Maxwell Farms skate park were cited for not wearing helmets. One of the individuals was stoked to discover that his police case number was 420.

Some people always try to trade you drugs for a ride.
I tell 'em, "3 joints are not going to pay my rent."

-Al, cabbie

CULTIVATING IN A CAR?

When a Sonoma police officer spotted a silver Chevy Prism with out-of-state license plates driving down West Spain Street at 8:55 p.m., he noticed the car had nonfunctioning brake lights so he pulled it over for a safety check. As soon as the driver rolled down the window the officer's well-trained olfactory senses detected the strong odor of fresh marijuana. The officer said to the driver, "I can smell marijuana. How much do you have?" First the driver denied having any marijuana, then he explained "some friends" had been smoking in his car. Nope, said the officer, I smell fresh marijuana. The officer removed the driver from the car and conducted a search, which led to the discovery of a large plastic bag in the trunk with 84 small marijuana plants inside. The 35-year-old driver, a resident of San Francisco, had no medical marijuana card, and if he had, it would have covered possession of only 11 plants. He was cited for cultivating marijuana and his portable garden was confiscated.

'PURPLE VOODOO' FOR A $1,000 LAPTOP

Patients in need of the healing balm provided by "Purple Voodoo," or "Blue Dream," or "Green Crack," or perhaps "Blueberry Haze" sometimes surf the website "budtrader.com" to find what one website poster described as "leftover AAA+++ medicine." A 22-year-old Sonoma "patient" turned to budtrader.com for a supply of such medicine and discovered a seller willing to provide some "meds" in exchange for a laptop computer and $300 in cash. Meeting in the Sonoma Safeway parking lot, buyer and seller agreed to the deal but the seller requested a

"A 22-year-old Sonoma 'patient' turned to budtrader.com for a supply."

ride to "his house" to get the medicine. He therefore got into the buyer's car and directed him to a house on France Street at Oak Lane. Taking the buyer's backpack with him, the seller said he would run into the house and come back with the medical herbs in a moment. He then walked through a gate beside the house and disappeared. The moment stretched into minutes, the buyer got suspicious, went to the gate and saw that it led to the back of the house and emptied onto an alley. The seller was nowhere to be seen, but a passing witness said he had seen the man running quickly southbound on Third Street East.

I was at this point where I wanted to do something good for someone else. I heard you could help at an old folks home. Go visit an old person and keep them company for an hour or so. So I went to the home and they assigned me this guy name Marvin. I meet him, and it's this guy in a wheel chair, who kind of looks like an old hippie with coke bottle glasses. So we hang out for a while. I see his room, and we stroll out to the patio and hang out for a bit.

"Weed man! Bring me some weed!"

Then it's time for me to leave. I give him my phone number and contact info, tell him I'll see him next week and ask him if there is anything I can do for him. Anything he needs? He looks up at me, while sitting in his wheelchair. He tugs on my shirt and in his raspy old voice, he says, "Weed man! Bring me some weed!" I'm not a pot smoker, but I know a few people who smoke. So, on the next visit I bring him a couple of joints. He's pretty excited about it. So, we hang out for an hour talking and then I leave. A few days later, I'm at work and it's really busy. One of the girls who answers the phone, comes up to me and tells me there is a call for me. It's a man named Marvin. I think, "Oh, I hope he's okay. He's calling me at work, so maybe something is wrong." I pick up the

*phone and I say, "Hey Marvin, how are you? Is every-
thing okay?" And in his gravely old voice, he says, "I'm
outta weed man! I'm outta weed! Get me some more
weed!" So that was the end of my time with Marvin. I
tried to do something good for people, and then I ended
up being a drug dealer at a convalescent hospital.*

-Otis, local

I'VE BEEN ROBBED; DON'T TELL

A resident of Fairview Drive reported that someone had stolen his
eight medical marijuana plants. The man wasn't willing to give deputies the names of any friends or potential suspects or cooperate in
any way. He even asked that the case not be reported to the media.

HOT BOX' PARTY ENDS BEFORE IT BEGINS

Some people call it a "hot box," others just refer to it as a portable
party. Whatever you call it, the point of the party is to fill a car up
with marijuana smoke to better share a toke. The fine print in party
instructions often gets overlooked: If your car is full of dope smoke,
only a dope plays the stereo loud enough to attract attention. Call
them what you will, on the night of March 20 three young men had
just settled into the cramped comforts of a Nissan parked outside
a residence on Second Street West when a citizen called police sometime past 10 p.m.

"The point of the party is to fill a car up with marijuana smoke to better share a toke."

after being alerted by the loud music emanating from the car. When
an officer arrived, the music was drifting through the doors and
three heads were visible inside. The officer knocked on the door, it
opened, and he asked what was going on. "Just hanging out," was
the reply from one of the three.

It quickly became clear the trio was hanging out with a glass marijuana pipe, some sort of clear plastic bong, a bottle of Southern
Comfort and a small amount of marijuana bud. Two of them also
had in their possession medical marijuana cards, although police
could not immediately ascertain the specific disabilities, chronic

pain or physical trauma for which they were treating themselves with the home remedy.

> *This girl got in the cab one night and immediately hunched over. I asked, "So what's up? Are you on probation or holding?" She said, "Both." I told her, "No worries, we'll get you to where you're going." That's our job. Regardless, we have to get people to where they need to go.*
>
> *-Gordon, cabbie*

When a Sonoma police officer stopped a car on Fifth Street West at Verano Avenue because of erratic behavior, the driver pulled up and over the curb before stopping. When the officer contacted the driver and noticed the smell of alcohol, slurred speech, unfocused eyes and other symptoms of intoxication, the driver insisted he had had nothing to drink and had taken no drugs. But he was having trouble keeping his eyes open and as the officer questioned him further he said, "OK, I smoked one bowl" of marijuana. The officer asked to look at the man's tongue, which was heavily coated green, and said it looked like the driver had smoked more than one pipe bowl of pot. The man became agitated and said, "I just told you, I smoked two bowls."

A PATIENT WITH POT

Police investigated a report of drug possession at a Broadway rehabilitation center and discovered the case involved a 32-year-old quadriplegic. A nursing assistant told officers there was an odor of marijuana in the room and that the patient did not have a medical marijuana card. Asked about the marijuana, the patient said it made him feel good. Visiting friends, he said, provided the pot and helped him smoke it. Police declined to cite the patient.

So when kids get caught with a joint or something, you aren't going to send them to juvenile hall, and you aren't going to slap them on the wrist. I think Sonoma does a great job of addressing misbehavior in a moderately punitive way, but without really f%*king up their education and prospects.

-Anderson, local

ANNUAL ARREST WINNER

Police signaled the winner of the annual Sonoma Arrest Derby, a fictional prize awarded by the media for the most arrests by one Sonoman in one year. The 32-year-old arrestee, picked up on a warrant in the Plaza, received his 11th arrest, beating out the runner-up by a margin of one trip to the county jail. He did not receive a trophy.

Historically, the cops don't aggressively enforce marijuana laws here.

-Anderson, local

A woman who was being charged with possession of drug paraphernalia even knew the penal code citation she was being charged with. A clerk on Sonoma Highway saw the woman drop a purse in some bushes and walk away. The clerk went out and checked the purse and discovered a meth pipe and the woman's identification. The deputy who responded knew who the woman was and figured she would be going to the Marina Center for dinner. The deputy was correct and waited until the woman was done eating and was walking outside. The deputy approached the 39-year-old woman and told her that somebody found her purse. The woman asked if anything illegal was found in the purse and the deputy told her there was. The woman asked if it was 11364 H&S, citing the California penal code for possession of drug paraphernalia. The deputy told her it was and cited her for possession of drug paraphernalia and being under the influence of a controlled substance.

LET'S KICK SOME ASS

Sonoma is where the Bear Flag Revolt happened and I guess some people are still revolting...against each other. I remember seeing fights after school at the graveyard, in the Plaza, and in many of the bars. Locals settling their business. I'm still very good friends with my buddy who I got in a fist fight with on the playground at Prestwood Elementary. He still mentions that the principal punished him more than me, because I was president of the 6th grade class. He's a Yoga Master now.

A local dentist reported Friday that a dissatisfied patient threw a set of dentures at him, hitting him on the head.

> *They had a huge fight going on, 50 or 60 people in the parking lot on Highway 12. I was on the motorcycle, a big 650, and didn't have any back up yet. So I came into the parking lot really hot, dropped the bike into a slide and knocked about 25 people down into a fence. Pretty much stopped the fight.*
>
> *-Officer Grey, Sonoma Police*

A guy with only five teeth reportedly bit another guy during a fight Friday night on Stolletti Drive.

It's like an old west town. There are a lot of fights.
-Anderson, local

It was nine against one during a fight at a Boyes Boulevard bar Wednesday night and the one was winning until his sister dragged him out of the tavern. Deputies questioned the patrons in the bar and everyone knew the guy, but, not surprisingly, no one could remember his name.

Sonoma is very accepting of eccentrics. I think it still is. Some of it's the Bear Flag mentality. We started this state. We will revolt whenever we frickin' feel like it.
-Anderson, local

A substation spokesman blamed the full moon for eight assaults in the Valley this week.

This dude from a reality show on MTV would come up from the city **"He got his ass kicked pretty quick."** *cause he was dating some girl up here. It was two years after his show. He was a total jackass. He was being really rude and asking us if we knew who he was, thinking he was really cool... and he got his ass kicked pretty quick.*
-Seth, local

A bloody-faced man was seen walking in the Plaza on Friday. When police approached the man, he said he didn't have any charges to file, since he had bloodied his face during a "mutual combat."

We were cruising into town. And we look over and see this guy in front of the bar, facing it, pissing on the front wall. Right there on the square. And it's Ted. We honk the horn. He turns around and gives us a thumbs-up, and he's got a black eye and half of his ear is chewed off.

-Seth, local

A disagreement over a parking space erupted Friday in Kenwood, prompting one 200-pound man to bump another with his belly. Deputies are submitting a formal complaint to the district attorney's office regarding the abdomen assault. A 61-year-old Kenwood man said he noticed the suspect pull into a space reserved for handicapped persons in the lot of the Kenwood **The angry man reportedly "shoved the victim with his stomach."** Shopping Center Friday afternoon. The man said he told the illegal parker of his mistake but was greeted with a barrage of hostile words and was challenged to a fight. The angry man reportedly "shoved the victim with his stomach." By the time officers arrived the belly bumper was gone, but deputies were given his license number.

Back in the day, we had our fights at the amphitheater in the plaza. The kids would sit in the seats and watch the fights. I had two fights there.

-Ted, local

A man reported to police late Friday that a guy named John grabbed his nose and shoulder on Second Street West.

It was a big party event in the square, and afterward, someone pushed some of the big dumpsters across the lawn and into the duck pond. People got so pissed off. Some locals found out who it was and kicked the s%*t out of the person. They policed it themselves. That's the blessing of living in a small town.

-Anderson, local

103

Neighbors told police that 50 kids were in Carter Park on Wednesday at 12:13 p.m. preparing to fight. Officers met up with some of the kids, who happened to be wearing boxing gloves. The matter was referred to Sonoma Valley High School administrators to handle.

> *The Bear Flag Revolt set the tone for all the quirkiness of Sonoma. You had a band of misfit soldiers, ragtag dudes, who are ready to start a fight. Getting ready to fight, take down General Vallejo and Vallejo invites them in and pours them tea, and gives them Sonoma. "Here take it. Just make me a senator." That's a funny beginning. We've been quirky since then.*
>
> *-David, local*

Drivers spotted a guy starting grass fires on Highway 12 Monday afternoon. The suspected arsonist told authorities he set the fires because he was "angry at himself, not the grass."

A man on Kenmare street claimed that some guy came up to him and said, "Do you think you're cool, do you think you can whip me?" and then proceeded to knock him down, causing a scrape on his leg

"Do you think your cool, do you think you can whip me?"

Tuesday. The victim said he'd never seen his assailant before and didn't know what would possess him to attack him.

> *We used to have a little van. That little van would literally circle the plaza and pick up drunks or people from fights, whatever, load 'em in the van. Haul 'em down to the police station.*
>
> *-Officer Reed, Sonoma Police*

Officers driving by the Blue Moon Saloon on West Spain Street noticed two women fighting in front of the establishment moments after midnight on New Year's Eve. Officers contacted the victim, a 28-year-old woman, who gave a vague description of her attacker, but when pressed for more details said, "What do you want, I'm hammered." The woman declined to press charges in the incident.

> *We were at the Sebastiani Theater, when there was a club up there. These guys showed up with crowbars and tire irons, and we had to draw our guns on them. I think they were surprised that we had guns. They turned around pretty quick. I don't think they were locals.*
>
> *-Officer Hamil, Sonoma Security*

DEPOT FIGHTS DRAWS MOB

A large group of Sonoma Valley High School students assembled in Depot Park last Friday afternoon to watch a 17-year-old and an 18-year-old duke it out. Police say they arrived at the park, which is just a few hundred yards from the police department, to find approximately 100 youths in a circle around the two combatants. As the officers approached, the group began to disperse and the two involved in the fight tried to walk away. Officers found them both, and delivered one to the hospital for vomiting. The fight appears to have been over an umbrella.

> *There used to be a lot of fights. Behind 7-Eleven was a good spot to watch a fight. There was always a beef in the park with kids-just teenagers not knowing what to do with their energy. It was usually 1-on-1 fights. I don't remember groups fighting or a group of guys beating up one person.*
>
> *-Seth, local*

PITCHER TAKES AIM AT UMP

The umpire of a softball game in Arnold Field told police that a player threw a softball at his head after he ejected him from the game. Police investigated and the player claimed that he was merely warming up to pitch for his team and was unaware that he was one of the players who had been ejected. The umpire later acknowledged that, since the ball had been thrown underhand and missed the umpire by several feet, the player's version of events was plausible.

> *The fights at the dikes were where we went if you got called out in Jr. High school. I never got to see any of the fights because I took the bus, and it left right after school. That kind of bummed me out.*
>
> *-Seth, local*

A Glen Ellen man reported that he tried to break up a fight between a man and a woman in the Plaza and was punched in the face. The man, concerned about the woman's safety, reportedly approached the quarreling couple and told the boyfriend, "Why don't you fight someone your own size?" The boyfriend took the man's advice and punched him in the face, knocking him to the ground.

MAN BITTEN AT LOCAL BAR

A man was recently bitten at a local bar after he allegedly punched his attacker twice in the mouth. According to police, Ray Housten, 26, of Sonoma, claims that his gnawing on the arm of fellow Sonoman Henry Scannell, 34, was done out

"A man was recently bitten at a local bar."

of self-defense rather than extreme hunger. Housten said that he saw an unknown man push Scannell from behind at the First Street West tavern at approximately 1:22 a.m. Friday, Dec. 28. Scannell swung around and looked at Housten, instead of the man who really pushed him. Scannell then punched Housten twice in the mouth. To defend himself, Housten grabbed what he believed to be Scannell's right arm and vigorously clamped down his teeth.

I must have been 21. My brother and I squared off in the plaza and duked it out. The cops showed up and looked at my drunk brother and said, "You look like you're half of the problem." I said, "I must be the other half. We're brothers!" Cop just shook his head and told us to go home. So we did.

-Kevin, local

Police received a report of a fight at the Sonoma Valley Veterans Memorial Building on First Street West, and found two 17-year-old males slightly bloodied, but with no serious injuries. The combatants explained that two friends of theirs had gotten into a fight earlier in the week, so they were, of course, trying to defend the honor of their respective buds - or something similarly noble. Medics arrived to examine the inconsequential wounds and, in a gesture of profound chivalry, neither lad chose to press charges against the other.

Most of the fistfights, especially around the Plaza area, are mostly teenage high schoolers. They find their rival and stuff like that. It's one of those things. They like fighting there, in my opinion, because I've made several suggestions to these groups over the years, I'd tell em, "You know, go out to Scagg's Island off of 37. By the time we hear about the fight you have, and by the time we respond out there, you guys can have your differences all resolved."

-Officer Jenkins, Sonoma Police

A SHOT OF TASER ON THE ROCKS?
An intoxicated man who refused to leave a saloon on Sonoma Highway ended up with a shot of Taser to go with whatever he was drinking, after he refused to leave the bar and started a fight in the process.

CHIEF TAKEN TOO LITERALLY, MAKES ARREST

Sonoma Police Chief Doug Jameson was minutes from his office, driving past the corner of First Street West and Napa Street around 5:10 p.m. on Aug. 6, when he saw two men scuffling on the sidewalk. According to the subsequent police report, the chief shouted at the men that he was a police officer and ordered them to "knock it off." Apparently misinterpreting the command, one of the men stopped, stood back, and then punched the other squarely in the face. The chief, who clearly was not suggesting a pugilistic tactic, intervened and cited the 25-year-old assailant for misdemeanor battery.

I had these two couples come into the bar at 11:30 a.m., and they were already drunk and really loud and obnoxious. They sit down at the bar. One of the guys tried to order, "Pitcher of margaritas, Chief!" I told him, "This is a family restaurant and it looks like you've already had too much." Well, he lunges at me across the bar. And on instinct I just grabbed the bottle of Galliano, that's the really tall bottle of liquor you see in bars, and I blurted out, "California state law says I can break this over your head if you get any closer to me." And that stopped him. I don't know how, because I totally made it up. His friend apologized and all of them left.

-Jeremy, local

THAT'S NOT YOURS

I was very excited to go on the Boy Scouts trip. It was the first Boy Scouts camping trip for me. I had all of my gear ready to go, but I didn't have batteries for my flashlight. I'm not sure why I didn't ask my parents for some. I thought I'd just casually walk into Longs and take what I needed. I was wearing my bright blue windbreaker. It was not a thick jacket. I found what I needed, four big D batteries. I thought I'd unwrap them so I could put two batteries in one pocket and two in the other. I proceeded to the checkout stand and bought a Jolly Rancher or something cheap like that. I made my way out of the store with two bulging pockets. Well, security busted me immediately and took me upstairs and called my mother while I cried. They didn't call the cops, but they scared me enough that I never stole again. I missed the trip. And my scouting career was short lived. I made a pretty dumb and odd choice on what to steal. I am happy to see I was not alone in this.

Another burglary from a vehicle on Melville Road. This time the thief took only one cassette tape from a stereo unit in the car. It was "The Beatles, 1967-1970," one of a two-tape set. The thief left behind "The Beatles, 1964-1966."

GRAMMA STOLEN FROM PIZZA PLACE

The owner of Gramma's Pizza reported that on Friday, June 18, someone stole a portrait of the mustachioed matriarch from the wall of his business. The owner said the portrait was there when he opened at 11 a.m., and he noticed it was missing when he closed around 10 p.m. The 14-by-18-inch photograph on canvas was valued at $200, and it is in fact a picture of the owner of the business—in drag.

> *The funniest ones are the ones that come in with these skin-tight jackets. And they try to stuff two big bottles of alcohol in them. Like you're not going to notice this extra baggage hanging off their sides.*
>
> *-Dan, store security*

A thief who calls himself "Crusader Rabbit" stole a portable ambulance radio from the Glen Ellen fire station on Arnold Drive between Tuesday afternoon and Wednesday morning, an emergency medical technician told deputies yesterday. The EMT said starting about 9 a.m. Wednesday, a young voice came over the radio calling "Help!" "Help!" Help!" and then started telling jokes on the air. "Why did the leopard get out of the shower? Because he lost his head and shoulders," was one joke he thought he heard, followed immediately by, "I'm right across the street from the station. Catch me if you can."

"A thief who calls himself 'Crusader Rabbit' stole a portable ambulance radio."

A woman appeared at the Valley Substation Monday morning and told deputies she wanted to clear her conscience of a crime committed by her boyfriend some time ago. She reported that the boyfriend had taken the valve stem cap off a school bus. When asked what they told the woman, a deputy said, "Nothing, they were laughing too hard."

The sheriff's deputies were always screwing around with police officers. In good fun. One time they went down to Bob Noble's Chevrolet. Somebody did not put the car keyboard away. That's the board that holds all of the keys for all of the cars. Well, someone went into every car and turned on all the emergency flashers and locked the cars. Hid the key board. Then they called us at the police department, from a pay phone to say that suspicious circumstances were going on down there. We show up, and every single car had its flashers on; doors locked. We couldn't figure it out. I found out later they were hiding across the street watching us and laughing, while we try to figure out what the hell happened.

-Officer Flynn, Sonoma Police

Saturday evening someone in a blue Datsun drove by a business on Highway 12 and grabbed the helium filled balloons decorating the entrance. A witness reported seeing balloons, valued at $60, held outside the car's window as it continued on its way.

BAD HAIRCUT LINKED TO BAD CHECKS
One Sonoma woman was arrested last week after more than $1900 in stolen and forged checks taken from the mailbox of a Sobre Vista Drive home were linked to her. Deputies say Tonya Wesler was taken to Sonoma County jail on suspicion of burglary and forgery after a Beno's Department Store employee who had accepted two checks for merchandise totaling more than $100.00 each was able to identify her after he remembered she was a former hairdresser who once gave him a bad haircut.

I rarely see people steal wine in the wine country. They usually steal liquor.

-Jacob, store security

Statues of Snow White and two of the dwarfs were stolen from the front of a home on Gable Street. The homeowner said she took the five remaining dwarfs inside for safekeeping.

A man told police Friday that his car had rear-ended another on First St. West near the post office, and when he went to offer the other driver some cash compensation for the damage, the man grabbed his entire wallet and fled the scene.

> *Halloween masked bandits stole masks through the mailbox slot at Tops and Trophys. They were going mailbox fishing.*
>
> *-Steve, local*

While waiting for his meat order to be filled at a deli counter of Fiesta Market Tuesday afternoon, a 26-year-old man ate cookies from the deli counter, a package of M&M candy and salad from the salad bar, worth a total of $1.20. After buying the meat, he walked out without paying for the other food he ate, the deputies said.

Sonoma Police received a report on Thursday that a large vibrator was stolen from a van parked on Austin Street.

> *Some people use their baby carriages to steal stuff. They pack stuff behind the baby in the carriage. The baby is lying down on the way into the store and baby is sitting straight up on the way out. They would have hundreds of dollars of items hidden behind the baby.*
>
> *Dan, store security*

Someone with a strong back and hearty appetite for barbeque stole a four-foot tall, 1,000-pound cast iron barbeque smoker from a Schellville delicatessen between Friday night and Saturday morning, deputies reported.

Sometimes I would be in charge of watching the entire shopping mall. I could be on my bike, which made me stealthier, and I had night vision, so I would catch people right in the act.

-Officer Hamil, Sonoma Security

VALLEY BURGLARS TAKE A VACATION

Area burglars seem to have taken the week off. Or maybe they were attending their national convention in Detroit, but they weren't on the job in the Sonoma Valley over the last few days. According to a sergeant at the Sonoma County Sheriff's Valley Substation, there were no burglaries reported to his office this week. "We usually average about one a day, so it's been real slow around here. It's very strange. I know we haven't caught all the burglars in the valley." The most serious crime of the week appears to have been committed at 3 a.m. Thursday when an unknown man grabbed a six-pack of beer from the 7-Eleven on West Napa Street and headed out the door. The crime was discovered to be a non-crime, however, when the clerk found $4 on the counter. The price on the six-pack was only $3 and the man left without his change.

It's against the law to steal State property. I've seen people at the Mission steal the prickly pears. That's the little cactus parts, with tons of **"I've seen people at** *needles. Instead of bust-* **the Mission steal the** *ing them, I feel justice is* **prickly pears."** *served when they try to reach into their purse to get it out. Guaranteed, those needles are going to stay in there for a while. They will never do it again.*

-Fredrick, Parks Employee

ONLY THE BEST FOR THESE DISCRIMINATING SHOPPERS

A Palo Alto couple with discerning taste traveled to Sonoma for a gourmet meal that they procured after some selective shopping and creative transfers at Sonoma Market. According to the police report, the pair entered the store at about 1 p.m. on April 15, gathered up both a shopping basket and a cart and proceeded through the aisles. Somewhere toward the back of the store they converged and transferred the items from cart and basket into a black bag which the man then carried directly out of the store and took with him into a car. The woman followed moments later but was stopped by the store security officer, who then directed the man to get out of the car and follow him back into the store. There the contents of the bag were examined and found to consist of a bottle of Napa Valley cabernet valued at $96.99; a bottle of Paul Hobbs cabernet, priced at $89.99; some smoked duck breast valued at $24.59; a packet of buffalo milk butter worth $6.99; and a slice of pizza valued at $2.99; for a total take of $221.55. The 65-year-old man and his 49-year-old companion offered no explanation for their dining selections. Both were cited for petty theft and released, minus the two outstanding cabernets, the smoked duck breast, the buffalo milk butter and the pizza slice.

I actually had very wealthy people steal. I'd ask them, "Why?" They'd open their wallet and have thousands of dollars in there, platinum cards, they're driving a nice car and then they're **"I actually had very** *stealing a candy bar,* **wealthy people steal."** *or something stupid like that. And I say, "Why would you do something like that?" And they tell me, "Well, just to see if I could get away with it."*

                                        -Jacob, store security

TEED-OFF GOLFER FILCHES FLAGS

Someone cut the 5th and 12th-green flags at the Sonoma Mission Inn Golf and Country Club during the night of Dec. 19-20. The reporting party told deputies that he was unsure if the miscreant had jumped the fence, or whether the perpetrator was "just a golfer angry at his putting."

An Agua Caliente man reported Wednesday that a pair of trousers he keeps under his bed are missing. Deputies have no suspects.

People like to use the cellphone trick. They walk out of the store while on the phone, and their pockets are bulging. They think everyone thinks they are talking to someone. I know they're not. They always use the cell phone as a distraction.

Dan, store security

THIEF DANCES OFF WITH BOOGIE BEER

Thieves made off with a "dancing beer can" display from a downtown delicatessen earlier this week. The bobbing, wiggling Coors Lite display was swiped from the front of the Sandy Creek Deli during a 30-minute period Sunday morning.

There was this rash of break-ins at the shopping center. They would crowbar their way in. I set up across the street late at night for a month, and finally, I caught this guy. When he pulled his hands out of his pockets, **After I finally cuff him, he asks me, "Do you think I can have a sandwich, maybe a cigarette before you take me in?"** *out fell some socks and batteries. I grab the guy and I can't bend his arm behind his back to cuff him. I had to fight this guy for 10 minutes, and I couldn't get his arm behind his back. Finally, I realize he's got a crowbar up* *the sleeve of his jacket. After I finally cuff him, he asks me, "Do you think I can have a sandwich, maybe a cigarette before you take me in?"*

-*Officer Hamil, Sonoma Security*

An El Verano resident told deputies this week that sometime during the last 25 years, someone stole his silverware. The 88-year-old man, who lives on Howell Avenue, said that 12-18 pieces of sterling silverware, valued at $1,500, are missing. The utensils were given to him as a wedding present in 1926 and the last time he saw them was in 1967 when he moved into the house.

Some people will rip open the diaper package in the store, change the baby in the isle and leave the dirty diaper on the shelf. Disgusting. People steal pacifiers a lot as well.

-*Dan, store security*

Two people were cited on trespassing charges after they were doing a Paul Bunyan imitation on Everingham Road Monday. Both, people from Petaluma, were found hauling off the wood they chopped.

THIEVES STEAL COPS' BIKE

Two Sonoma police officers had their bicycles stolen around 11:30 p.m. Saturday as they were breaking up a party of juveniles on Prairie Way. After breaking up the party, the officers returned to where they had left their bicycles and found them missing. One of the pair of $650 mountain bikes was later recovered in a nearby bush, but the other one, as well as the bicycle thieves, remains at large.

Someone stole a six-foot-high statue of a half-man, half-dolphin from a business on East Napa Street. The theft was discovered and reported last Tuesday around noon.

I decided we should dig up some olive trees. You could seriously make some money from this. If you try to buy a mature olive tree it would cost a lot. Well, I would dig 'em up and sell them on craigslist for $500. I had this van that I rented from some tweaker in Sonoma. So, we were coming past the dump with 6 trees in the back, and a cop rolls up on us and lights us up because I had fake tags on the van. I used Microsoft Word to print the month and the year. He was pretty pissed about it. While he's busting me he asks what the hell is up with the trees in the back of the van and busts me on that as well. So I go to jail for 5 days. It sucked. I made some good money off olive trees.

-Elliot, local

POLICE BIKE RETURNED --IN PIECES

The $650 police mountain bike stolen from outside a party is being returned to the Sonoma Police Department, piece by piece. Two officers' bicycles were stolen from the front of a home on Prairie Way, while the officers were responding to a party of juveniles. They were both unlocked. One bicycle was quickly recovered from a nearby bush, but the other bicycle remained missing. This week, as the investigation into the theft continues, pieces of the bicycle have been returned to police. So far, the frame, tires and saddlebags of the bicycle have been returned in good condition. No arrests have been made.

WOMEN DISCOVER CLUES TO INTRUDER'S IDENTITY

Workers at a CPA's office on Third Street West reported that someone had broken a window and entered the office over the weekend of May 8-9. The only thing the intruder appeared to have stolen was a can of juice. The office workers-all of whom are women-offered police a clue when they reported that the toilet seat in the bathroom had been left up, leading them to conclude the intruder was a man.

People used to pump before they paid. One girl who worked here averaged 3 drive-offs a week. Pump number 6 and 8 you can't see really well. So as soon as it got busy, they'd pump the gas and peel out without paying.

Max, gas station attendant

BURGLURY SUSPECT CRAVES CHOCOLATE

A 19-year-old man couldn't resist his need for chocolate when he walked into the Chocolate Cow and took candy without paying for it. He told officers that he was hungry for candy but didn't have any money.

If somebody steals and they're sorry for it, I'll make 'em pay for the item and give them a second chance. But if they do it again, [they] don't get a third chance.

-Jacob, store security

THIEVES RIP OFF FOOD LOCKER, YET AGAIN

Clearly indicating they are onto a good thing, a thief or thieves returned like bears to honey for their third illicit visit to a food locker outside the Cornerstone Café at Cornerstone Gardens on Arnold Drive. Their first visit occurred last February, when they made off with numerous chilled tasties, perhaps in preparation for Valentine's Day. In November, a week before Thanksgiving, the locker was illegally reopened and someone took $500 worth of hams and cheeses. Then, during the night of Friday, Dec. 29, presumably in preparation for a gala New Year's Eve bash, someone went back to the same locker and took $2,000 worth of packaged meats, hams and turkeys. Sheriff's deputies continue to investigate the thefts while watching their calendars for the next festive holiday. Valentine's Day, of course, is Feb. 14, and Chinese New Year follows on Feb. 18.

My thing was: anybody who's out after 2 a.m. was usually up to no good. Unless it's a drunk stumbling home, in which case, I'd usually give them a ride home.

-Officer Hamil, Sonoma Security

PRECIOUS METALS

There's a reason every penny minted since 1983 is 97.5 percent zinc, with a thin copper coating. That's because copper is now too valuable to be used in copper pennies. Before 1982, pennies were 95 percent copper, which means that a copper penny today is worth 2.5 cents. And it also means that the 300 pounds of copper sheeting, along with 60 pounds of aluminum sheets, that a Sonoma man left in the bed of his pickup truck overnight on Patten Street near First Street East, is now gone.

HO HO OH NO!

Christmas time used to mean, "Who's going to steal baby Jesus?" When there was a Nativity scene in front of City Hall it was pretty common for the statues to go missing every holiday season. You would hear people talking about the missing members of the scene while they shopped at the grocery store. I remember seeing Joseph lying on a bench in front of Steiner's bar in the mornings. People find weird ways of dealing with holiday stress.

A 32-year-old Sonoma man, found singing "Little Drummer Boy" in the driveway of an Arnold Drive residence at 10:30 p.m. on Saturday, was arrested for disturbing the peace. Deputies, responding to a call of an unruly individual at a party, found the suspect dancing and singing in front of the house. He reportedly ignored deputies' requests to stop and was taken into custody.

A citizen reported seeing a "suspicious-looking Santa" in the area of Grove Street and Verano Avenue Monday morning.

> *We had this one kid who we caught stealing one of the figures in the nativity scene in front of City Hall, and as punishment, we made him guard the nativity scene for a bunch of hours for a few nights. We got him a raincoat and a hat, so he could sit there on a bench and guard it. That was the judge's punishment.*
>
> *-Officer Thomas, Sonoma Police*

The statue of baby Jesus was returned to the manger scene in the plaza sometime Christmas Eve.

Residents reported seeing legs hanging out of a dumpster on Fifth Street West on Thanksgiving morning. Officers found a 47-year-old man inside sleeping.

> *I remember one Christmas someone had moved the wise men from the nativity scene in front of City Hall across the street in front of the bank ATM. One wise man was at the ATM, and the other two were in line behind him.*
>
> *-Ann, local*

Deputies found a nice elderly man with a bit "too much Christmas cheer" wandering around attempting to hitch hike late Wednesday. They took him to a nearby coffee shop to warm up.

POLICE INVESTIGATE THEFT OF THE WISEMAN FROM THE CRECHE SCENE

The black king has been stolen from the crèche scene on West Spain Street. Members of the Sonoma Valley Ministerial Association told Sonoma Police Tuesday that the figurine of Balthazar was taken sometime between Friday evening and Sunday afternoon. It is valued at $800. The missing member of the trio of wise men stood about 4 feet tall.

For several weeks, people had been calling about this deer. Middle of the day, out on their front lawn, eating in the front lawn or eating their flowers, and he was a very healthy-looking young buck. Well, he got hit on Fifth Street West, and the people said he was still alive. By the time the animal control officer got out there, the deer was dead, but the officer didn't know what to do with him. I said, "Well, if you can get him loaded in the back of the truck, bring him on down to the station." He would have to do that anyway, either that or get city crew out there to deal with it. They got it loaded in the back of the truck, and brought it down to the station. I told him how to hang it up in our new kennel that **"That Christmas we made the biggest pot of stew."** *had a cement floor and a drain and everything. We had some guys doing work in the back, community service for misdemeanors. Well, one was a guy I grew up with, I knew he knew how to hunt and everything, and he gave the officer a hand and they got [the deer] pulled up over the drain, cut its throat, skinned it out and everything. After work that night, I went home and got some sheets. We hung the deer in the men's locker room because they didn't use the showers in the men's locker room. It was so freezing icy-cold back there, nobody could stand to shower. So we hung it in the shower that night and the next day, we aired it again. Eventually we put knives down, cut that sucker up. We cut him up into stew, and froze it for Christmas, which was only a couple months away. That Christmas we made the biggest pot of stew. The Chief went down and bought 10-pound bags of potatoes and carrots and everything. We made a humungous big stew, got the French bread and everything. So for Christmas that year deputies, highway patrols, everyone*

could come in and have a hot meal… so the joke was
"roadkill stew" and a lot of them KNEW it was.
-Officer Reed, Sonoma Police

A large group of juveniles were reportedly "running at large" in the 500 block of Este Madera Friday night. Police caught up to the group to learn they were Christmas carolers.

It was Christmas morning and I watch this girl throw this
glass at this guy's face. Blood everywhere. 'Tis the season.
-Rob, local

Four men were reportedly throwing snowballs at cars driving by the Plaza the evening of Dec. 20. Police told them to knock it off.

RETURN TO SENDER; NINE POUNDS OF CHRISTMAS POT

When a Sonoma resident came home from an out-of-town trip he discovered a notice of an attempt to deliver a package. Retrieving a brown cardboard box from the post office, the man saw that it had been sent to an address in Patchogue, N.Y. Marked undeliverable by the Patchogue post office, it was sent to the return address, which was hand-lettered with the man's name and the street address of his home on First Street West, but the handwriting was not his. According to the postmark, the package had been sent from Santa Rosa. The man took the mystery parcel home, opened it and saw, covered by a dark-colored sweatshirt and cushioned on the sides by a towel, seven packages wrapped in Christmas paper. Each package was about a foot long, 10 inches wide and four inches thick. The man called his grown children to see if they knew anything about the presents, but they didn't. So on December 24, he tore the Christmas paper off one end of a package, saw that the contents were tightly wrapped with plastic and promptly called police. The responding officer noted that the packages felt "spongy," cut through the plastic on the partially opened package and was immediately greeted by the familiar musky odor of a green, leafy substance sometimes worth upward of $3,000 a pound on the street. That package weighed 1 pound, 5 ounces, so the seven packages together approximated something over nine pounds. Depending on quality and location, a pound of good marijuana can sell for between $1,600 and $3,400, at least in Sacramento, according to an ostensibly knowledgeable poster on cannabis. com. Another poster claims consumers can pay up to $6,500 for a pound of "da bombdiggity," a qualitative term apparently unfamiliar to law enforcement officers who generally assign a lower value to confiscated cannabis. Local law enforcement is apparently unfamiliar with "da bombdiggity," but whatever the value of the Sonoma recipient's anonymous and presumably unintended gift, his honesty secured the appreciation of Sonoma police who said that, from what they can determine, whoever mailed the package from Santa Rosa pulled a Sonoma return address out of the phone book and got the delivery address wrong.

There was a deputy that used to work the valley here, he's retired now, and there was a fire in a mobile home in the Boyes Springs area. It was a single mother with a couple of kids, and she was robbed. It was Christmastime. Christmas gifts were taken, and she had two small children, and one of the deputies knew that she was an honest person, and she didn't have enough money to replace the gifts. One of them was a Cabbage Patch doll. It was back at that time, and he was in the station talking to me because the deputy was married to my niece. He was going to go out and try to buy a couple of things for the kids and was talking about a Cabbage Patch doll and couldn't find them. I said, "Let me call my niece, she works at Longs." Called down there. That year Longs only got a couple of Cabbage Patch dolls, and they had a drawing for them, and my niece won it. She was in her early twenties... so I told her what the deal was. She said every year for Christmas at Long's they would fill up a couple of shopping carts, one for Marines, one for the fire department or Salvation Army, Marines and something else. She said the Marines haven't picked theirs up yet, and she donated the Cabbage Patch doll, and I got to pick out perfume and stuff for the mother and picked out some stuff for the little boys and this deputy picked everything up and took it to the woman. There was a nice big article in the paper about him.

-Officer Reed, Sonoma Police

A Grinch swiped a bicycle worth $100 on Christmas Day from a front yard on Barrett Avenue in Boyes Hot Springs.

It was the night after Christmas, and I remember watching a giant brawl across the street from the cheese factory. On the lawn, in the street, had to be at least 20 people. A guy I know asked me to hold his dog for him, so I held the leash, while he crossed the street and jumped into the fight.

-Andrew, local

A small plywood baby Jesus wrapped in a white dish towel was stolen from a nativity scene in the front yard of a home on Salten Street Sunday night. Frosty the Snowman was knocked over, as well, but survived.

On my day off, I went and grabbed a Christmas tree for one of my regulars. I tied it on top of my little car and brought it over to her house. She wouldn't be able to do it, so I wanted to help her out.

-Kevin, cabbie

An overly ambitious shoplifter left the Lucky supermarket at Maxwell Village with a six-ounce pack of sliced salami stuffed in his pants and an apparent yen for something more substantial to take home for the holidays. He therefore picked up a Christmas tree from the lot in front of the store and began hefting it across the parking lot. The store manager gave chase, thereby initiating a brief race handicapped significantly against the thief for obvious reasons. Had he made good his escape, the would-be tree thief might have become a local legend, but as it **"He displayed unmistakable signs of intoxication, which may have explained his impulse to filch the Yule tree."** was he was apprehended by the manager and returned to the store where arriving police discovered he was on probation. One condition of the man's probation was that he not consume alcohol, but when police interviewed him he displayed unmistakable signs of intoxication, which may have explained his impulse to filch the Yule tree. Because he was able to recover both the tree and the salami, the store manager did not press charges.

A Christmas bag full of bullets was turned into the Sonoma Police Department for destruction.

> *Think about it. If you put the crib scene in the middle of the plaza and you have 4 bars, closing at 2 in the morning, and the people leaving the bars are walking through the Plaza...some crazy stuff is bound to happen.*
> *-Officer Jenkins, Sonoma Police*

A 25-year-old woman in a 1998 Chevy Camaro, who told police she was a transient, was clocked speeding on West Napa and was pulled over in the parking lot of the Chevron gas station. When police contacted the driver and asked if she knew how fast she was going, she replied, "About five over." She then apologized and said she was in a hurry to get to her boyfriend's house for Christmas Eve. When the officer pointed out Christmas Eve was more than three days ago, she said, "I meant New Years Eve." The officer then explained that New Years Eve was still three days away and the driver then re-corrected herself, saying, "I meant for the holiday." Asked if she'd been drinking, she acknowledged consuming one glass of wine. Asked if she had a suspended driver's license or was on probation, she said "no" on both counts. The officer then ran a records check and quickly discovered that she had no driver's license and was on a three-year probation for a prior DUI. And a preliminary breath test revealed a BAC of .12.

ASPIRING CRIMINALS

We used to hide in the graveyard after school and water balloon the school buses. If you could make it in the window it was considered a bullseye. It was all in good fun, according to us. One time, one of the buses slammed on its brakes and this young driver bolted out of the bus. He caught one of us, because he was so fast. Scared the heck out of us. We learned our leasson and avoided his bus from then on. Sometimes you just start young. Small town. Small crimes. Small Kids.

Police got a report that a small boy was darting in and out of traffic in the 100 block of West Spain Street Tuesday morning. Officers found a boy matching the description being severely "chastised by mom."

A self-conscious 13-year-old boy was caught stealing $5 worth of Binaca spray from Longs. The teen was sighted and placed in the custody of his mother.

An 8-year-old boy was caught stealing plastic action figures and a pacifier from Safeway, Friday.

We had a kid in custody one time for arson. Eric Stack, another officer, got this weird thing from his mother for Christmas. It was one of those weird toy guns that lights up, different colors, and makes all those sounds. He went into the cell where the kid was and he asked him, " You know anything about that arson?" Kid said, "No, I don't know anything about it at all." So, Eric pulls out **"It's a truth gun, if you lie to me, it's gonna tell me."** *this toy and points it at him. Kid says, "What's that?" Eric says, "It's a truth gun, If you lie to me, it's gonna tell me. Did you set that fire?" "No!" And Eric pulls the trigger and it makes this woop woop woop sound and he's says, "We got you!" And kid says, "You can't use that, it's illegal!!!!"*

-Officer Clayton, Sonoma Police

Police received a report Friday afternoon that Prestwood Elementary School students were "out of control," rocking a school bus in front of the campus. Officers said they could not find any problems when they arrived at the school.

Someone called police at about 4:30 p.m. on Thursday to say three kids were standing in front of a hair salon on Sonoma Highway with a knife. Police checked it out and discovered that the "knife" was really just a comb.

Three boys, 12-13 were arrested and charged with attempting to steal a car from Sonoma Ford last Thursday.

I put a stink bomb in a police car when I was a kid here. That was up at the vets' building.

-Officer Thomas, Sonoma Police

THIEVES ROBBED

Two boys, 11 and 12, confessed to Sonoma Police Monday that they walked into a classroom at Prestwood School last week and stole a saxophone. The trouble is, someone stole it from them. The two youths were cited for the theft and the police are still looking for the sax.

Wednesday morning, the station received a call from the manager of Exxon on Broadway, who reported he found a 3-year-old youngster waddling down the street in his pajamas. The youngster had apparently figured out how to unlock his front door and went for an early morning stroll while mom and dad were not looking. Parents and child were united at the scene.

Two small boys were darting back and forth through traffic Sunday afternoon on First Street East and Spain Street.

Police received an anonymous call that two kids, ages 8 and 10, were riding their bikes into Maxwell Village early Tuesday afternoon. The caller wondered why they weren't in school. Officers talked to the kids and learned they stayed home sick from school and to top it off, one boy was taking his little sister out to lunch for her birthday. Their mother was called.

> *I'd stop some kids being nuts in a car. I'd just call their folks at home and tell them, "When Jonny gets home, you might want to have a chat with him." That was it. That's what we used to do here, but that's all changed now.*
> *-Officer Thomas, Sonoma Police*

Police received reports that a "gang" was hanging out in the Sonoma Marketplace late Thursday. As it turned out, the "gang" was a group of four boys, ages 10-12, waiting for their mothers.

Three children ages 7, 9, 10 were admonished Saturday for annoying ducks.

Officers received a report Sunday afternoon that three kids were goofing off in the roadway near Quik Stop on Broadway. Apparently one boy was lying in the road while two others held a sign reading "for free." Officers contacted the kids and told them to stay off the road.

COPS SAY SCOUTS WEREN'T DOING A GOOD DEED
Someone kept calling the "911" emergency line on Friday evening and hanging up. The calls were soon traced to the Vintage House senior center on First Street East, where a Cub Scout meeting was taking place—and police discovered a few of the boys were playing with the phones. The kids were admonished.

WHERE THE HELL AM I?

It's a small town, but people still get lost. And drinking doesn't help. The general rule is...if you don't know where you are, you've probably had more than enough wine!

I had a guy on Boyes Blvd, just around the S-turns there, sitting with his car parked and 50 feet of chain link fence dragged behind his truck, passed out behind the wheel with a fifth of Jack Daniels in his lap, and the car running. I went to make contact with him as I called for CHP, and he looked at me and says, "aw, nah nah, I'm in my house. I'm sleeping." **"He said he went to his car to drink, and that was the last thing he remembers."** *And I go, "Dude. You've got fifty feet of fence behind you." So, CHP got there and said, "Where did you follow him from?" I said, "I didn't follow him from anywhere. It's obvious that the guy is drunk, and he's got fifty feet of fence dragging behind his car." They asked him where he lived, and he said "Santa Rosa." They said, "You know where you are?" He said, "Santa Rosa." "No, you're in Sonoma. Where did the fence come from?" He goes, "What fence?" I swear the fence was fifty feet long* *trailing from behind. To this day, I don't know where it came from. I don't think they ever found where it came from. They looked all over the neighborhoods and stuff, and they couldn't find where it came from. The guy didn't know how he got there. He said he wasn't drunk driving. He said he went to his car to drink, and that was the last thing he remembers.*

-Officer Hamil, Sonoma Security

A Sonoma police officer noticed a male figure lying on the grass on the east side of the duck pond, his face aligned with a pool of vomit. When asked if he was OK, the recumbent figure replied, "Yeah, except that I 'm (bleeping) drunk." The officer then asked why he was lying there on the ground. "I was camouflaging myself so I could sleep," the man explained. "By the way," he added, pointing to the mess on the ground, "don't ever drink Corona." As it turned out, the sot had two outstanding arrest warrants and was summarily booked into the county jail.

I had a drunk driver one night that was up at Maxwell Park, and she was on the sidewalk. Parked on the sidewalk! I pulled up behind her in my patrol car and asked her if she needed some help. She said "No, No! I'm just driving to the store." I **"She said that her attorney** *said, "You* **told her that if she ate some** *realize you* **Mentos, then she could drive."** *are on the sidewalk?" She said, "No, no, no, no, I'm just driving." I said, "You think you can make it to the shopping center?" So, she went down to the shopping center, and I pulled in behind her and got on the radio and called the station and told him I've got a deuce. It was really funny because she didn't know where she was,*

and she said that her attorney told her that if she ate some Mentos, then she could drive while she was drunk.
-Officer Hamil, Sonoma Security

Two people ran from a car after it collided with a dumpster on East Spain Street. Michael Terry was arrested on suspicion of public intoxication after he returned to the car. According to the witness, Terry said he was "too drunk to know who was with him and too drunk to know who was driving."

My mom worked dispatch for a while. People would call up in the morning to get a cab, so they could use the cab to find their car. They were so drunk; they couldn't remember where they parked their car the night before. That happened quite a bit.
-Amy, local

BEER ME

When we were in high school my buddies and I stole a couple of empty kegs from behind a restaurant in town. We kept them in my friend's parent's back yard. Anytime we wanted to have a party, we could find a local to fill the keg and never had to put down a deposit. We weren't rocket scientists, but we knew how to meet our budget. Yes, it's wine country, but who doesn't love a "cold one"? Or 12 pack? Or in our case, a keg?

While most people were still having their morning coffee, deputies found a man sitting in a field on Sonoma Highway enjoying his morning 40-a slang term for a 40-ounce bottle of inexpensive, fortified beer

> *I used to carry sacks in the back of the patrol car. And when I caught kids out drinking I'd make 'em clean up the whole area. I'd tell them to fill the sacks up with all the cans, bottles, and trash and then to go home and have their dad call me. That was their punishment.*
>
> *-Officer Flynn, Sonoma Police*

THE ENDURING POPULARITY OF TWO BEERS

It is standard police protocol when questioning a motorist suspected of driving under the influence of alcohol, to ask, "How much have you had to drink?" By remarkable coincidence, and with amazing consistency, a majority of drivers appear to respond to the question with precisely the same answer: "About two beers." Breaking down the answer word-by-word may offer insight into its popularity. "About" suggests a level of protective imprecision. If subsequent evidence contradicts the answer, "about" provides a useful fudge-factor. "Two" is generally a safe number of drinks, unless the driver weighs 65 pounds, and offers the benefit of being both candidly confessional and explaining the presence of booze breath. "Beers" generally contain the least amount of alcohol by volume (although one beer may be six or eight times the volume of a single shot of Old Overholt) and therefore sound to the inebriated driver like a less serious intoxicant.

Given the popularity of this standard answer, a Sonoma police officer can be pardoned for the shock he must have felt when he stopped a red Cadillac DeVille around 9:40 p.m. on March 8 as it failed to yield to pedestrians in the crosswalk at First Street West and West Napa Street. When he posed the standard question to the 24-year-old Sonoma man behind the wheel, the young driver abruptly cut him off with the statement, "Sorry sir, **"Sorry Sir, but can we skip the formality of the sobriety tests. I've had way too much to be driving."** but can we skip the formality of the sobriety tests. I've had way too much to be driving." With continued candor, the motorist further confessed he had been imbibing at not one, but two of the Plaza's more popular watering holes.

We'd knock out boards in the fence behind the super-market. When they delivered the beer, we would get a line going, like a bucket brigade, and steal beer, carry it through the fence, put the boards back in the fence and keep our beer in that field. We'd leave it there all weekend and go to the field to replenish.

-Jared, local

A LITTLE FRIENDLY BEER ADVICE

A friendly 60-year-old man outside the Sonoma Safeway store was the third person snared in a decoy sting. The amiable man told a decoy couple he could get in trouble for buying them beer, then sat down on the curb with them and gave them a friendly lecture on quality beer, advising against the cheap suds they asked him to buy. Ultimately the man entered the store, bought the six-pack, then walked around the corner of the store and left the beer in a clump of bushes. Police, who witnessed the transaction, then arrested the man for buying alcohol for a minor.

There are a few good open fields to drink beer in. They have multiple exit spots, so you can see people coming from a number of directions and get out without getting busted.

-Jared, local

SONOMA POLICE TAP KEG IN RECORD TIME

Sonoma police caught a group of juveniles with a cold keg of beer just 16 minutes after it left Albertsons last Friday. At 3:16 p.m. April 29, officers spotted a group of about 20 juveniles in the 400 block of Lovall Valley Road. One of the five cars parked at that location was a blue Chevy Nova, which officers recognized from previous reports involving juveniles purchasing alcohol. Officers asked the 18-year-old driver to pop the trunk, and there lay the iced, untapped keg of beer. The young man admitted he paid a man in the Plaza to purchase the beer for him, and Albertsons reported that the keg was purchased at 3 p.m.

BREAKFAST BREW IN A BAG

A 40-year-old Boyes Hot Springs man was enjoying a breakfast beer in a black plastic bag when an officer spotted the 40-in-a-sack and cited him for drinking in public.

> *Steve was key. We would party out at Watmaugh and 5th. Probably have about 15 cars way out there, drinking beer and hanging on the side of the road. We were so far out and you could hear a car coming a quarter of a mile away. Steve was a mechanic in town on the weekends. He knew the sound of a Ford cruiser (The cars the cops drove). So if we heard a car, everyone would stop talking, Steve would listen, and you'd either here him say, "Cops!" and you'd jump in your car and split or "All good!" and you'd crack another beer.*
>
> *-Andrew, local*

A teen beer bash was busted up by deputies who were patrolling on a routine security check on Millerick road in Schellville, late Sunday night. Deputies spotted a huge bonfire and upon approaching the area, saw approximately 15 teenagers scatter in all directions. At the scene they found two kegs of beer. The beer was taken to the substation until someone claims ownership.

> *I was having this massive party at my parents place and when the cops showed up, it was at its peak. My mom was cooking hamburgers, we had a water main break in the front yard, water shooting 50 feet the air, a guy with a huge laughing gas whip-it container, a lot of kegs, a band playing in the back yard and hundreds of people. That was a wild night.*
>
> *-Jared, local*

How many beers have you had? Answer: "a couple."
They still use that answer today.

-Officer Jenkins, Sonoma Police

Deputies spotted a man wearing a plaid shirt hiding in the bushes in Maxwell Farms Park. After he failed to respond to their commands, deputies moved in and found that it was not a man at all, but a plaid shirt covering a full, cold keg of beer. The keg was confiscated.

The cops were making us pour out our beer one night, and in the middle of doing it, one of them said "Hold on!" He reached over and took a sip of the beer he was having me pour out. I was so mad, but what could I do, they were letting us off with a warning so we didn't say anything.

-Greg, local

SIGN OF THE BEAST

I've been chased by dogs, cornered by a cow, and when
I was on a Boys Club camping trip at Sugarloaf Park,
a skunk sprayed my tent. I actually took deodorant out
of my bag, wiped it across the space between my upper
lip and nose and slept like a baby. I was made fun of, but
I had the best night sleep of all the campers. Some locals
have been chased by other animals and some people are
busy stealing stuffed ones.

A Ribbon Circle resident complained Monday that she was being
attacked by ants.

Officers received a call from the manager of Plaza Del Sol Apartments that he had a large, exotic and extremely nasty bird "cornered" in his swimming pool area. Officers responded and found
a male Ringneck Pheasant, which fit the description in this week's
Index-Tribune Lost and Found section, which read. "Lost: One
Ringneck pheasant...extremely aggressive." "You got that right,"
was the report from the responding officer. The bird and his owner
were reunited at the police station.

> *We had this officer who was going up Norrbom Road, and there was a skunk. He got out of his car, and the skunk started to chase him. Well, he jumps up on his patrol car and starts shooting at the skunk, but misses. He ran out of ammunition. He had a '38. So there he was, stuck there on top of his patrol car.*
>
> *-Officer Thomas, Sonoma Police*

An eastside resident complained Wednesday that her neighbor's cat bit her for the fourth time. Officers said the cat bit her because he was trapped in her garage, along with several other neighborhood cats. They were all liberated.

A stuffed animal was taken from a residence on Orange Ave. The burglar gained entry by prying open a window and tearing a screen. Juveniles are suspected.

ROOSTER SPOOKS WOMAN

A woman reported an aggressive rooster on West Spain Street at 4:30 p.m., Wednesday, according to the Sonoma Police Department. As the woman checked her mail, she heard a ruffling in nearby bushes. A white rooster emerged and began to follow the woman in an intimidating manner. No attack took place.

Someone removed a 100-pound owl from atop a 10-foot post on Hyde Rd. on June 3.

> *There was a Golden Bear at the Golden Bear Lodge in Kenwood; the big bear was on top of the sign. That thing was sto-* **"I just saw the Golden Bear** *len a number* **on the back of a truck."** *of times, and one of the times, we got a call at the police station and*

a person said, "I just saw The Golden Bear on the back of a truck going through Sonoma!" And this was like 2 o'clock in the morning or something.

-*Officer Reed, Sonoma Police*

PLASTIC COW SLOWS TRAFFIC

A large plastic cow blocked traffic in the roadway of the 300 block of East MacArthur Street on the morning Sunday, April 1. An unidentified passerby alerted the Sonoma Police Department to the cow at 7:52 a.m. Officers responded, removed the obstruction and brought it to police headquarters. The cow was later determined to belong to "The Cows in Sonoma Valley," an art project that displays the ornamental cows at various locations in order to market them for later auction.

Killer pigeons were spotted knocking "big chunks" off a roof on East Napa Street Saturday afternoon.

A theft took place at the London Lodge saloon in the 13700 block of Arnold Drive at about 2 a.m. on Nov. 25. A man reportedly took a mounted deer head off the wall, claiming it was his.

WHERE'S THE BEEF? COW GETS KIDNAPPED AGAIN

Someone out there is having a cow, because Angie has been kidnapped again. The life-sized fiberglass cow has stood stolidly for about 30 years atop the roof of Angelo's Wine Country Deli on Highway 121, southeast of Sonoma. But now it's missing, and the owner is bewildered as to why anyone-even a beef thief-would want a 50-pound, red and white plastic cow. "It's something you can't hide too easy, you know what I mean?" said the owner, who owns the cow and the building that houses the deli. The theft was first noticed last Sunday-not by the deli employees, who apparently take old Angie for granted so much that at first they didn't even notice she was gone-but by customers, who view the bovine as a cherished landmark.

A woman called the sheriff's department Thursday afternoon to report finding two 26-inch aluminum giraffes hidden in the bushes adjacent to the driveway of her Agua Caliente Road home. No reports of stolen giraffes have been found, deputies said. The aluminum animals have been stored in the sheriff's property section.

> *There were wild pigs up in hills of Sonoma. There have always been some wild pigs around the area. Boy, they could be very destructive. My dad worked on the hospital grounds and there were a couple of areas that he had to watch when he got out* **"A big old boar would** *of the Jeep because* **take on a Jeep."** *of the pigs. A big old boar would take on a Jeep. If it got mad or you were in its territory, it'd come after you.*
>
> *-Officer Reed, Sonoma Police*

A hungry dog got the best of a prowler late Friday on Glenwood Drive. A resident there heard a man yell, "Get away from me," followed by a loud crash. Deputies looked over the backyard fence and came eye-to-eye with a "big" dog who looked like he just enjoyed a snake.

PURLOINED BRUIN FOUND IN CREEK
One of the several carved bears that decorate the Black Bear Diner at the corner of Second Street West and West Napa Street, which have been the focus of so much attention this summer, attracted some unwanted interest when it was stolen on the night of Sunday Sept. 1, according to a report by the Sonoma Police Department. Police had no leads in finding the bear valued at $2,000, but the case came to a quick end when children playing in Fryer Creek near Manor Drive found the bear stuffed in a culvert later that week.

Three teen-aged boys reportedly attempted to steal a three-foot-tall, stuffed white rabbit from PayLess Drug Store on Easter Sunday.

The bear that was in front of the Swiss Hotel for years was a real bear that had been hit by a car in Yellowstone. This guy had it stuffed and gave it to the owner of the Swiss Hotel.

-Miles, local

A stuffed 4-1/2-foot-long iguana valued at $75 was reported missing from an apartment complex's garden area.

A citizen reported a "black bear" in the creek near Brookside Mobile Home Park late Sunday evening. The bear turned out to be a black Angus bull that had wandered from his pasture. Sonoma officers chased the bull (and were chased) around the area of West Napa Street and West Spain Street until Freddie Wallace arrived on the scene to assist them by opening a spot in the fence to his pasture.

HIGH SCHOOLED

Most likely to Succeed? Class Clown? Most Creative? Most likely to get caught smoking weed out of an apple in the creek? Please vote today.

A teacher at Sonoma Valley High School reported that someone had inserted glue into the locks in a number of the doors at the school, an annual senior prank.

> *My girlfriend's mom bought a scanner when we were in high school, so she could look out for us. We were at this party out at Skaggs Island, and my girlfriend looks at me and tells me we have to go because she just got a text from her mom. "Cops are on the way." Sure enough, as we are driving back on 37, near Sears Point, 3 police cars go flying past us. We got out of a few situations with the help of her mom.*
>
> *-Frank, local*

A visitor to the high-school campus reported that several students picked up and moved his car in the south parking lot the morning of March 27. No damage was done by the prank.

I used to call the principal "buns" because he wore such tight pants. He didn't like that much.

-Russell, local

MOONER GETS CHILLY RECEPTION, TICKET AT ARNOLD FIELD

Immediately following Montgomery High School's last minute, 21-20 football win against Sonoma Valley High on Nov. 17, a 17-year-old Santa Rosa boy expressed his delight by walking out to Arnold Field's 30-yard line, dropping his trousers, and exposing his rear end to the home team fans. Local fans replied by summoning police, who cited the boy at 10:22 p.m. for indecent exposure.

At the high school the fights were out near the Quonset hut. One of the teachers would break up the fight. If it was Mr. Tabish , you'd get a referral. If it was Mr. Hartstein, he would threaten you with being suspended, but there were two teachers who were ass-kickers. They took care of business. If they broke up the fight, they'd give you the look that said, "If **"The officer, having had some experience with youth and apples, recognized the intended purpose of the hole as a marijuana bong."** *I catch you doing this again, I'LL kick your ass." And everyone believed it, so if they caught you fighting you usually wouldn't get into another fight.*

-Russell, local

AN APPLE A DAY

When five juveniles were spotted wandering off campus during class time at Sonoma Valley High School, the school resource officer was alerted and soon detected the sound of adolescent voices emanating from the bed of Nathanson Creek. As the officer came within view, he saw one youth holding an apple that he quickly tossed into a blackberry bush. Because throwing the apple into the bush could constitute littering, the resourceful officer had reason to direct the young man to retrieve the fabled fruit. When he did, after some prickly effort, it was discovered to have a neat bore hole through and through. The officer, having had some experience with youth and apples, recognized the intended purpose of the hole as a marijuana bong. He then asked the dreaded next question; so, if this is a bong, who's got the weed? There was a very long pause, and then one of the five reluctantly added he did, and produced a plastic bag with four buds. The bong boy and the bud boy, ages 15 and 17, also coughed up a pack of cigarettes, a joint and two cigarette lighters and were cited for being minors in possession of cigarettes and minors in possession of marijuana on school grounds. The other three were released.

Two students at Sonoma Valley High School reported that someone "B.A.ed" them Tuesday.

> *One time all these kids had a huge beer party up on Thornsberry Road. So sheriffs, CHP, and us all went up there to bust it up. We parked way down the road and crept up there, but one of our guys tripped and hit something and the kids scattered. Some got away, but every car that was left there, we had towed into town. Maybe 10 or 15 cars. We had court at the high school, in Golton Hall; the judge was on the stage and kids had to bring their parents to get their cars released. The kids would go on stage to meet the Judge, get cited, and the parents would be in the audience.*
>
> *-Officer Thomas, Sonoma Police*

Senior pranksters turned on fire hydrants at the high school and flooded the tennis courts early Thursday morning. Those responsible are facing disciplinary action by the school district.

They could separate the sheep from the goats. They knew who was going to be trouble and who wasn't. The police knew all the kids by face. They would cruise through the high school and get to know the kids. Just hanging out. Not being confrontational. I don't think the police ever had malicious intent. Overall, I felt the police were concerned and friendly.

-Amy, local

JUNK FOOD LOVERS TAUNT HIGH SCHOOL

Pranksters switched flags at Sonoma Valley High School this week, replacing "Old Glory" with a McDonalds banner Saturday. As soon as the joke was discovered, the colorful flag was taken down and returned to its owner.

WHAT MARIJUANA? OH THAT MARIJUANA.

It was 9:45 a.m. on Wednesday, a nice morning for a stroll along the Nathanson Creek pathway, and two teens were enjoying the fresh air as they walked south toward an observant adult who noticed them before they noticed him. The adult noticed the two 15-year-olds because, at that time on that day, they were supposed to be in class. And he noticed them because he was the school's resource officer, and it is his job to notice such things. But it was not until the lads were within 30 yards of the officer that his presence actually registered on them, at which point they came to a simultaneous dead stop and, as if choreographed by an unseen hand, pivoted 180 degrees and began walking hastily in the opposite direction. A campus supervisor intercepted the truant twosome and escorted them to the school office. There the officer conducted the obligatory backpack search, which revealed a pipe bowl. During the search, the searchee kept his hands nervously around the front of his pants, leading the officer to then search the lad's pockets, which were empty. The officer then delicately and judiciously inspected the now-suspect's waistband, but still found nothing. He therefore grasped the boys belt loops, instructed him to jump up and down and jiggled firmly on the loops until something dropped to the ground. The contraband object turned out to be a yellow highlighter, which the officer uncapped to discover the insides had been removed and replaced with 1.3 grams of marijuana.

Six live turkeys were found inside the main building at Sonoma Valley High School Monday, June 1. They were held until Animal Control officers could respond and remove the birds.

The cops busted this party in high school one night. It wasn't our house. I was DJing. We brought the kegs. We brought the stereo. There must have been 300 people. The parents were out of town for the night, and it was crazy. The cops showed up and started busting the party up. Well, we booked it from the party and never got caught. Over the back fence and out of there. The next day I went back to get my stereo and the kid's dad is there. He said, "Oh, this is your stereo... I'm keeping it." And he did, for a while. I got it back a little bit after that.

-Russell, local

CAPTAIN OBVIOUS

I've learned it's stupid to drink in the plaza before 11 a.m. I've learned not to write your full name in cement and I've learned that you probably don't want to party on the lawn in front of the police station. Sometimes some of the best advice is not from Dear Abby, but from police reports that point out the obvious.

A resident of West Spain Street looked out her window Thursday night to see a group of boys pushing her BMW automobile down her driveway. The woman stopped the thieves, but neglected to call police until the next day because she didn't want to do the paperwork. She was advised to call police right away if she finds someone trying to steal her car again.

> *He had his full first name and his last initials spray painted on the building. In blue. It wasn't too hard to find the kid in the system. We go to his house, and he still had blue paint on his fingers.*
>
> *-Officer Gregerson, Sonoma Police*

DARWIN SAYS, DRUGS IN CAR, DRIVE QUIETLY

It was what some observers might have described as a Darwinian moment Jan. 14, when police pulled over a gray, 1984 Chevy Caprice in which the entire rear seat had been removed to make room for an enormous speaker system. The Caprice being a very large car to begin with, the custom stereo system was capable of making serious sound. So serious that it quickly attracted police attention at 5:12 p.m., as did the tinted windows. State law prohibits motorists from playing music audible past 50 feet, so for anyone not wishing to draw attention, that would presumably be a good rule to obey. The Caprice driver was not so inclined, however, and he further aroused

"State law prohibits motorists from playing music audible past 50 feet, so for anyone not wishing to draw attention, that would presumably be a good rule to obey."

police curiosity by blurting repeatedly, "Please don't tow my car, please don't tow my car," and by the continuous ringing of his cell phone.

Because the driver was on searchable probation, police went through the Caprice, but found nothing suspicious. But guessing that there was more there than met the eye, they called in a K-9 unit and utilized the sensitive nose of a highly trained dog to examine the vehicle once again. The dog quickly "alerted" to a spot under the car's dash where police found a digital meth scale and a pill bottle wrapped in black electrical tape. Inside the bottle were four plastic bags containing a total of half an ounce of methamphetamine. A series of text messages on the driver's cell phone further clarified the purposes of the bagged meth. One read, "Wouldn't hurt to ask ... any chance I can get some and pay you tomorrow?" Another read, "That stuff is good, it's real good..." Arrested for transporting a controlled substance, possessing a controlled substance for sale, possessing a hypodermic syringe and violation of probation, was 41-year-old Dean Slattery, of Sonoma, who was booked into the county jail.

Officers asked dispatch to explain to the woman the meaning of the word "emergency."

-*Officer Reed, Sonoma Police*

TRANSPORTING STOLEN GOODS 101

A required course for anyone developing the curriculum at Crime Tech University would have to be "Transporting and hiding stolen goods, 101." It's a course that would have been helpful for a 32-year-old Petaluma woman who was stopped by a Sonoma police officer at about 10:30 a.m. on Monday, March 14, on Broadway near Andrieux Street when he noticed that her grey, 2001 Volvo sedan had a smashed windshield. Contacting the driver, the officer asked for her license. She said she had recently lost it. He then asked for her name and the name of her passenger, who was out of earshot. She told him her name was Carol Melissa Fry and that her passenger was simply, "Anita." She didn't know the woman's last name. Then the officer asked the passenger what her name was and the passenger gave an entirely different and, as it turned out, real name. Armed with probable cause, the officer spotted a small purse in the car with a bankcard inside bearing the name Noel Palmer. The officer then did a records search, learned that Noel Palmer was the listed owner of the vehicle, and had a photo of Noel Palmer sent to his cell phone. When the photo arrived he compared it to the driver and was not enormously surprised to find that they matched. Lesson Number One: When you lie to a police officer

"Lesson Number One: When you lie to a police officer about your name-and your passenger's name-it is wise to have some credible back-up identification handy."

about your name - and your passenger's name - it is wise to have some credible back-up identification handy. It is also handy to have your ID match the name on your auto registration. Since doing this is beyond the skill, imagination and resource of all but the top tier of professional criminals, it is best not to lie about your name. In addition to her real name, the officer also learned that Palmer's driver's license was suspended and she was on felony probation. That warranted a search of the car, which revealed a plethora of property, along with items of U.S. mail addressed to two different men, neither of whom was Noel Palmer. Lesson Number Two: It is unwise to drive about in broad daylight, on felony probation, in a car with a smashed windshield filled with various valuable items and pieces of mail that do not belong to you.

> **"Lesson Number Two: It is unwise to drive about in broad daylight, on felony probation, in a car with a smashed window filled with various valuable items and pieces of mail that do not belong to you."**

A detective was called in to assess the contents of the car, which included a white, stand-up portable air conditioner, an orange Skill saw, a flat screen TV, a DVD player, a shop light and a Famous Stars hat. She was booked into the county jail under her own name.

There was this local, Warren, who would always call the restaurant on the Square and order take-out. I would have to take it over to the guy, and he would never tip. Never. Ever. So, he calls and orders one night, and I tell him it will be about 20 minutes, and he says, "If you can get some poor schlep to deliver it that would be great." I say, "a schlep, Warren?" He says, "Ah, you have to come to New York sometime and you would know what I'm talking about." I said, "Well Warren, I'm from New Jersey, and I still don't know what you're talking about." He says, "Well, a schlep is someone who would bring that over to me." I said, "No, Warren, that's not a schlep, that's a schmuck." After that he always came by to pick up his food. I feel I out-yiddished him.

-Otis, local

LESSONS LEARNED ON LATE NIGHT BIKE RIDE

It is not a good idea to be riding your bike at night without lights - especially at 2 a.m. And if you do, by chance, ride your bike without lights at 2 a.m., you should probably consider leaving your methamphetamine at home. And if you don't leave your methamphetamine at home, you should probably not crash into a Sheriff's patrol car. And if you should happen to crash your bicycle, without lights, at 2 a.m., into a Sheriff's patrol car, you should probably not argue with the deputy sheriff inside the patrol car about whether or not you should get off the bike and submit to questioning. The deputy shined a spotlight on the bicyclist and discovered the rider also had no brakes when he crashed into the patrol car.

"911, what's your emergency?" "My car was broken into 3 weeks ago." That's not an emergency.
                                                Officer Reed, Sonoma Police

SONOMA PLAZA GOING TO THE DOGS

There are signs posted and police patrols, but the message that dogs are not allowed in the Plaza, even on a leash, hasn't seemed to penetrate the consciousness of some local residents. That was the case on the evening of Tuesday, Aug. 21, when police received word of a dogfight behind City Hall. When an officer arrived he found what appeared to be an injured dog and a man carrying a 40-ounce can of malt liquor. The dog, a shepherd mix, was on a leash, and the malt liquor appeared to have been significantly consumed. The owner of both became instantly confrontational when the officer arrived and told him dogs weren't allowed in the Plaza and the prohibition was posted. Employing a popular obscenity, the man said he didn't see any *#*# signs, and added that his dog had just been attacked by another dog. The man said he had tried to break up the fight and suffered minor injuries in the process. The officer determined that the man appeared to have consumed enough malt liquor or other intoxicants to produce the clear signs of alcohol intoxication and took the man to the side of the Plaza to continue their discussion about the presence or absence of "No Dogs in Plaza" signs.

The dog showed no visible tags and when the officer asked the man for the dog's **"The man didn't want to reveal the dog's name."**

name, the man said, "I don't know." Pressed further the man said he didn't want to reveal the dog's name because, "It's a work in progress." After having the man's minor injuries evaluated by a Sonoma Fire Department EMT, the dog owner was charged with being drunk in public, having a dog in the park, and having a dog without a license.

> *I remember I bought a lighter at Albertson's when I was 17, and by the time I got home the checker had called and told my mom. As soon as I walked through the door she said, "Hand over the lighter."*
>
> *-Andrew, local*

On May 1, according to a clerk at the Boyes Food Center on Sonoma Highway, a man entered the store, snatched a $45 bottle of Patron Tequila, and ran. The clerk chased the man but could not catch him. The next day, the man-who-likes-good-liquor returned, and this time he grabbed a bottle of Hennessy cognac, apparently assuming if you've outrun someone once, you can always do it again. But this time the clerk was quicker. He grabbed the speedy booze-hound before he could escape, and called the law. When deputies arrived, the would-be cognac connoisseur confessed, "I thought I could do it again. I guess I got a little greedy."

A 49-year-old Sonoma resident went to the Sonoma Police Department at about 11 a.m. on Tuesday, Nov. 24 to file a report. While there, the officer at the counter recognized the woman as someone whose driver's license had been suspended. The officer called the department's traffic officer. The traffic officer parked just down the street from the police department, and pulled the woman over as she drove by. The woman was transported to Sonoma County Jail and charged with driving with a suspended license.

When Maxwell Park became a park, they made it a no-drinking park. I used to go into there and bust the drunks there. I'd tell them, "You should go in the city limits, drop down to the Plaza. You know, as long as you guys aren't being buttheads or being drunk, you can drink all day long if you want." Then, they started doing that, and then we had a problem down there.

-Officer Jenkins, Sonoma Police

POLICE LOOK INTO THEFT OF FOUR "DONUT" SIGNS
Four signs bearing a very philosophical saying were taken from a Broadway art studio, it was reported Sunday morning. The four signs, which were each four feet by four inches, read; "As you travel the road of life keep this first among your goals, while you like to eat the donuts you must also accept the holes." Police are looking for the signs.

PLEASE DON'T SMOKE AT THE PLAT
Offering teenagers advice is a risky business. Most of them have an uncanny ability to detect the faintest trace of anything hypocritical, insincere, patronizing or just stupid. They also have a tendency to think that in their brief but intense tenure on earth they have managed to acquire more wisdom and common sense then people decades older. And while many of them express the belief they will die young - i.e. under 50, perhaps because they can't imagine ever being that old - they have the paradoxical belief that, in the meantime, they are essentially invincible. That allows them to drive cars recklessly, consume dangerous amounts of almost everything - including alcohol - climb cliffs, jump off bridges, and tempt fate in other crazy or creative ways. The problem with offering them advice is further compounded by the fact that much of what we tell them not to do, we have done ourselves. And they know it. And finally, when we instruct

them on how to live in this world, and they look at how we have lived in this world - at monumental lapses of integrity in business and politics, at the war, poverty and environmental chaos with which we have set their table - they may well be excused for asking who we are to advise them. And yet we must, because they are our children and they don't really know as much as they think they do. That said, here is some unsolicited advice to Valley teens, most of whom will never read it. It is of- **"For more than 40 years it has been** fered in ad- **used as the unofficial, top-secret,** vance of the usual high **don't-tell-anyone place that every-** school gradu- **one knows about."** ation pronouncements because we want to address the recent Cinco de Mayo party up on the Plat. The Plat, in case you have no Sonoma teenagers and were never one yourself, is an extraordinary site high atop the city, just off the Overlook Trail above Mountain Cemetery. For more than 40 years it has been used as the unofficial, top-secret, don't-tell-anyone place that everyone knows about, where you can go, hang out, drink beer and, in general, party. But it is more than just a party place with unrivaled views across the Sonoma Valley. It is also a miniature Machu Pichu where generations of teenagers have constructed labyrinths of stone, walls, paths, passageways, benches, miniature arenas and windbreaks with the precision of professional masons. And despite periodic parties, they generally manage to keep the place spotlessly clean. On the evening of May 5, however, a large number of teens celebrated at the Plat, during which they consumed a lot of beer (illegally) and smoked a lot of cigarettes (dangerously and probably illegally). We know this because Sonoma police officers, alerted by noise audible on the Plaza, investigated and detained at least 45. The revelers accessed the Plat through a 5-foot hole cut (illegally) in the cemetery's perimeter fence. It may well be that nothing will stop teenagers from drinking beer. It can be argued that the Plat is a better place to do it than someplace requiring vehicular access, although police will continue to enforce the law, as they should, even if it's just shoveling water with forks. But cutting the cemetery fence is serious vandalism, and smoking cigarettes and leaving the butts in the dry tinder of that hillside is an invitation to tragedy. So here is some very simple, easy-to-follow advice: If you go to the Plat, don't smoke. And please stop cutting the fence. There are other ways to get there.

> *I tried to start an illegal casino in the back of this bar, because they had 3 or 4 apartments behind the place. So my grand idea was to start an underground casino in Sonoma. I bought these two slot machines and put them in this back apartment and I thought I'd be raking in the dough. Nope. They were always breaking down and they didn't accept dollars and it was a total bust. I really thought it was going to take off.*
>
> *-Nick, local*

LESSON: NOT IN YOUR OWN COMPLEX

If you're going to break into a coin-operated washing machine, it would probably behoove you not to do it in the building in which you live. That revelation probably came a bit late to a Boyes Hot Springs resident **"The revelation probably came a bit late to a Boyes Hot Springs resident who might now be eligible for a Darwin Award."** who might now be eligible for a Darwin Award. It was Wednesday, at a little after noon, when sheriff's deputies were called to a five-unit apartment complex to investigate a vandalism report. The owner of the property told the deputies he had gone to check out a washing machine when he found the machine flipped upside down with somebody hunched over it.

The property owner asked the man what he was doing, since he didn't appear to be repairing the machine or washing his clothes. With remarkable candor the man replied, "Getting coins" and, without looking back, handed the owner part of the coin box. When the suspect finally turned and saw who he was talking to, he took off and ran to one of the apartments. It did not, therefore, take deputies an excessive amount of detective work to locate the suspect. They simply knocked on the apartment and arrested him on felony charges of burglary.

> *A common thing is to take the product out of the package and then put it in their pocket and then it's a matter of proving that the product is ours, because they can claim it's from somewhere else.*
>
> *-Dan, store security*

FIRST APPLY FOR JOB, THEN STEAL SOMETHING

A woman, whose job prospects at Sonoma Market took a sudden nosedive after she filled out an application form, turned in the form and promptly went to the nutrition counter where she pocketed a sponge scrubber and some Vita Coconut water, then left the store. Confronted in the parking lot by the store security officer, the woman became argumentative. When police arrived she was placed in handcuffs, while explaining that because her husband had not given her any money that morning, she had taken the coconut water so her kids "would have something to drink." Because she would not provide a name and had no ID, she was booked into the county jail for petty theft.

A Sonoma police officer had barely mounted his bicycle outside the police station at the corner of Patten Street and First Street East when a car came cruising down First Street with a loud stereo system booming out music audible well beyond the legal 50-foot limit. The officer flagged the car down and instantly smelled the unmistakable odor of fresh marijuana. The driver, a 25-year-old Sonoma man, grudgingly produced a small amount of marijuana and a glass-smoking pipe with residue in it. The officer charged the driver for possession of less than one ounce of marijuana and possession of drug paraphernalia. He did not charge the driver with astoundingly bad judgment for driving a car with excessively loud music past a police station while smoking marijuana.

I had people walking right past me with a basket full of stuff, and I have a t-shirt on that says, "Loss Prevention." I'm like, "Really?" I'd just wait for them to go out the door and then grab them and grab the cart and bring them back inside and say, "What are you doing?" They tell me, "Well, I didn't think you'd notice." I'd ask them, "I wouldn't notice that you've got a cart full of meat going out the door?"

-Dan, store security

TELL A LIE: GET A FREE RIDE TO JAIL

Psychologists have a name for; it's called existential guilt. You don't feel guilty because you've done something wrong, you feel guilty because you think you are wrong, existentially, systemically, independent of any bad behavior. That may have been the mindset of a passenger riding in a car that was stopped at 1:30 p.m. by a sheriff's deputy on Verano Avenue. The deputy pulled the car over because the passenger wasn't wearing a seat belt. When he asked the passenger for his name and age, the passenger, a 44-year-old Valley resident, lied. He gave a false name and a false age, and the deputy, who was well-seasoned in such conversations, detected a false note. Further questioning **"He gave a false name and a false age, and the deputy, who was well-seasoned in such conversation, detected a false note."** produced a different name and a different age and the new name belonged to a man who was on felony parole. He wasn't wanted for anything. He wasn't known to have committed any recent crime. He wasn't drinking or high on drugs. He was just on parole. Giving false identification to a police officer, however, is a crime. So in the time it took for an inborn psychological impulse to frame a false answer to a simple question, the man went from being guilty of nothing more than failing to buckle his seat belt - at worst a minor citation - to committing a crime that violated the terms of his parole. The man was arrested for parole violation and booked into the Sonoma County jail.

NO "HOME FREE" FOR DUI SUSPECT

A 58-year-old El Verano resident apparently thought he was home free Tuesday, March 18, for reaching his own driveway safely after traveling for several blocks with a police car on his tail and a staggering amount of alcohol in his body. A police officer first spotted the man in an Audi at about 1 a.m. drifting between lanes on Riverside Drive. With the officer right behind, the Audi rolled through a stop sign at 10 miles an hour. The officer put his red light on but the Audi continued through another stop sign before pulling into a driveway. The man stumbled out of his car, dropped his keys, leaned on the Audi for balance and announced, "I'm home." That news didn't dissuade the officer from conducting a field sobriety test, which the man failed. A subsequent breath test revealed a preliminary blood alcohol level of .30, more than three times the legal limit. The heavily intoxicated driver explained he had consumed three beers at one Plaza saloon, followed by two brandies and a beer at a second establishment. He expressed the opinion that he should be given a break for making it home. He was booked.

STATION IDENTIFICATION

I've always wanted to know what goes on behind the scenes at the police station. Given that every day, officers work hard to protect the community and risk their lives, I was surprised that police officers are some of funniest people I've met. I guess when you have such a serious job, you have to let a little steam off once in a while.

> *At the old police department, we had one bathroom for men and women, and the door was a little high off the floor so there was a pretty big gap. When someone was in there, one of the officers would come in with the little lady finger fire crackers, light 'em, and toss them under the door. It was a good group of guys to work with.*
> *-Officer Thomas, Sonoma Police*

A small brown teddy bear is in protective custody at the sheriff's station while his owner is in the county jail.

SINGING BIRD FLIES INTO COPS' HEARTS

They're whistling while they work over at the Sonoma Police station. A colorful exotic bird, taken into custody earlier this week, is adding a little (high-pitched) music to the world of local law enforcement. The vivid bird flew into the Sonoma Rental Center on Highway 12, where he was apprehended by police. Now he remains perched in the department's dispatch office, waiting for his owner to claim him. So that his owner can properly identify the bird, police officials do not want to reveal too much about his look or the types of tunes he belts out. He is such a wonderful addition that police said they were surprised that his owner has not come forth.

Back in the day, we would bust up so many parties: 2 deputies and 400 kids. We'd have to bust the kids, take their beer and send them on their way. We'd confiscate a lot of beer. Well, that would get backed up at the substation, so you'd often find yourself able to have a beer and watch a movie at the substation after your shift was over. It was a nice perk. I'm sure they don't do that these days.
-Officer Clayton, Sonoma Police

Two men came into the police station Sunday. One was handcuffed and needed help in being freed. Police assisted.

One of our dispatchers lived over on First Street, and he'd walk to work at night. Well, there had been snowfall in the mountains that day, way up there, and two of the officers went up and brought back a load of snow. When this dispatcher walked to work that night, they **"Chased him the rest of the way to the station throwing snowballs at him."** *waylaid him and chased him the rest of the way to the*

station throwing snowballs at him. By the time he got to the station he was pretty wet.

-Officer Reed, Sonoma Police

One of the deputies reported Saturday night that cockroaches four inches long are invading the Valley substation.

When we first moved to the new police office, we had a camera in the back lot, where we kept our cars. It moved around, and **"And the chief looks at me** *you could* **and says, "I don't even want** *zoom in if* **to know." And he went back** *need be. We* **to his office."** *knew Fred was going home for dinner. So, anyway, we go out to the police car that we know he's going to take home and we flip all the switches to the "On" positions. Everything: the wipers, lights, sirens, radio, overhead lights. So, we're all in dispatch watching the cameras, and the chief walks in and asks, "What's going on?" I said, "Just watch." So, Fred gets in the car, gets settled, flips the key and everything turns on, and he's scrambling like crazy to get everything off. And the chief looks at me and says, "I don't even want to know." And he went back to his office.*

-Officer Flynn, Sonoma Police

Deputies have been "hot under the collar" for several days because the air conditioning unit at the substation has been not working properly. Investigation into the cause of the problem is continuing, deputies said.

A large cookie box filled with miscellaneous ammunition was turned into the police department for destruction.

When other deputies from other areas would come down to the valley and work overtime, they'd be impressed. They said, "You know, I can't believe how many people wave to you guys. And they're using all five fingers."

-*Officer Jenkins, Sonoma Police*

ALLEGED POT GROWER ARRESTED AT STATION

In what was probably one of the easier collars recently performed by local law enforcement, an El Verano man went to the sheriff's valley substation to inquire about a warrant and was promptly arrested.

Years before, when they didn't have a dispatch here, they had a red light on a pole in front of City Hall. And if you got a police call, the operator at Sonoma State Hospital handled it and dispatched you. You'd see the light on the pole light up and you would call in. Well, one night they couldn't get a hold of the operator, so they drove out there to see what was going on, and she was on the floor with some guy just having a good time together. That's why she didn't respond to the radio.

-*Officer Thomas, Sonoma Police*

COPS NOW OWN 'JAIL BIRD' MASCOT

Sonoma Police now "officially" own the multi-colored parrot that was turned over to the department officials several weeks ago. Donations from police employees, which amounted to $100, were turned over to the man who found the bird. Still nameless, the feisty feathered character has become the chirpin', dancing mascot of the department. In fact, the Sonoma Police Department recently purchased the bird a spacious, sophisticated new cage, as well as numerous toys, "exotic" birdseed and various beak paraphernalia. There will be no more junk food for the burly bird. A sign on his cage warns that he can no longer eat pizza, french fries or chips. It's only healthy stuff from here on in, said one employee.

There were a lot of things you wouldn't be able to get away with now. During the swing shift, from 1 a.m. until 2 a.m., there would only be two guys on shift.
                                    -Officer Jenkins, Sonoma Police

A citizen who had read in this column about the appearance of cockroaches at the Valley substation gave the deputies a jar of boric acid powder last week. The janitor has sprinkled the powder around the floors of the substation and deputies said there have been no more sightings of the four-inch creatures. Boric acid is supposed to be lethal to cockroaches but not as toxic to humans and pets as some other methods of pest control, deputies said.

One of the officers used to walk to work. One night, he was coming in at 7 o'clock. So we put a closed sign on the front door of the police station, turned off all the lights and hid in the building. He walks up to the door, and he's looking through the windows confused as heck, and we are laughing quietly, hiding. And he's wandering around the front of the building wondering what the hell is with the closed sign. Finally, he walks in and we turn on the lights, jump up and start laughing.
                                    Officer Flynn, Sonoma Police

A woman called police Wednesday to report she heard their department mascot parrot singing (in the background) over her scanner. She suggested they name their new feathered-friend "Happy" or "Joy." The bird is still nameless.

We used to have explorer scouts. There was a mom and pop mausoleum on the ground level up there at the cemetery on the hill. Someone had broken into the crypt and pulled open the casket. Well Warren Bishop, one of the other officers, found it open and looked in and noticed the body was pretty well preserved. I get a call to come up to cemetery and I **"Come on Billy, he won't** *have this explorer* **hurt you. He's dead."** *scout, Billy, with me. We get up there, meet up with Warren, and Billy is standing back quite a bit, and I say, "Come on Billy, he won't hurt you. He's dead." He's like 16 years old and we are in the middle of the cemetery. So Billy starts walking up to the to the crypt, pretty close and Warren, who is the first to go in, says, "Oh my god!" And Billy stops dead in his tracks and says, "What?" And Warren says, "It looks like it was opened from the inside!!!" And this kid ran back, as fast as he could, to the patrol car.*

-Officer Flynn, Sonoma Police

First, it was cockroaches fought with boric acid. But then deputies at the Valley substation found black widow spiders. Deputies had been collecting the unwelcome spiders into a coffee can recently. The evidence proved to be sufficient to get a pest control company out to spray the substation this week.

I would start the day off with the 4th of July parade on the Square in the morning, go to the pillow-fights in Kenwood until that got over at 6 or 7 o'clock, and then come back downtown for the fireworks. So, I was working from 6 in the morning until almost one o'clock that night.

-Officer Jenkins, Sonoma Police

A sleeping bag, motorcycle helmet and a duffel bag filled with food and charcoal were left Monday on the doorstep of the Valley substation. Deputies stored the items in a closet and stuck the hamburger in the refrigerator "so it won't stink when it rots."

*I think there are three types of people in law enforce-
ment. You have the do-gooders, trying to help folks. They
always get in trouble helping folks. You've got the person
who wants to bash heads, and you have the guy who just
fell into it looking for a job. That last guy is the best, because he doesn't have an agenda.*

-Officer Flynn, Sonoma Police

An injured pigeon was brought to the police Tuesday.

*I remember there was this kid who was getting into trou-
ble. We thought we had turned him around because he
became an explorer with the fire department. Well, a ways
into that we discovered that he had been setting fires with
another kid. Twenty years later I was at a party and I
look across the room and make eye contact with the kid.
He comes up to
me and asks me if
I'm Jim Clayton,
and I say, " Yes."
I'm not sure how*
**"I just wanted to shake
your hand and say thank
you because you helped
me turn my life around."**
*it's going to go... you never do in those situations. The
guy then puts his hand out and says, " I just wanted to
shake your hand and say thank you because you helped
me turn my life around. I'm married now with a couple
of kids and I've been sober for years." He thanked me
for making a difference. It was cool. It's not often that
you get to see the payoff of your job.*

-Officer Clayton, Sonoma Police

A man turned in to the police department for destruction a bayonet
he bought in the Philippines during World War II.

> *He ended up falling asleep on a bench right there in the plaza, so we pulled up real slow in the patrol car and got a couple a feet away, and then we hit the siren! Oh man, scared the heck out of him.*
>
> *-Officer Thomas, Sonoma Police*

Finally, officer Doc Emerson has chicken pox. Department management is telling those who worked with him during his contagious stage to "sweat it out," while they wait for the virus to incubate. "If you are feeling "fowl," said the daily log, "you will know why."

> *There was a bunch of kids in a car going really slow and blocking a fire truck with its lights on, on the way to a fire. The kids were laughing because they thought it was funny. I pulled them over and gave the driver a ticket: failure to yield to an emergency vehicle. Well, this kid was mad as hell. The kid says, "I want to talk to your boss." I said, "He's*
>
> ## "I want to talk to your boss!"
>
> *up at the department." The kid says, "Well I'm going up there right now." I said, "Be my guest." He gets in his car and leaves. I get in my car and leave. I pull into the back lot of the station and go through the back door. I hear the front door bell ring. It's the same kid. He says, "I want to talk to your boss." I said, "You're talking to him." He says, "I want to talk to the chief." I said, "You're talking to him. What can I do for you?" He got so mad and stormed out.*
>
> *-Officer Flynn, Sonoma Police*

KNOCK KNOCK

My brother and I once tried to sell people flowers door to door. The problem was, we would pick the flowers from the yard of the person we were trying to sell to. We weren't the smartest 8-year-old entrepreneurs. You never know who's going to knock on your door, could be a religious person, could be someone needing a phone, could be a drunk person dressed up in a clown suit needing to use your bathroom. You just never know.

WHOSE HOUSE IS THIS, ANYWAY?

Not the dead of night- when the stranger arrived at the front door of a house on Dixie Canyon Circle. When the resident opened the door, the stranger stepped inside and promptly urinated on the living room carpet. The stranger appeared to be more than a little inebriated. Understandably unhappy with the intrusion, the resident ushered the stranger out of his home and called police. The stranger, meanwhile, went straight to the bed of the resident's pick-up truck, parked just outside the home, climbed into the truck's open bed and went to sleep. When police arrived they found the stranger, still asleep, in the back of the truck. Awakened - literally - by the long arm of the law, the heavily intoxicated 18-year-old from Sonoma explained he thought he was at a friend's house.

Neighbors reported seeing two men going door to door offering religious advice without, however, disclosing their religious affiliation.

> *We would toilet paper this guy's house on a regular basis.*
> *We'd t.p. the whole place, lawn, bushes, trees- the whole*
> *place caked with toilet paper. Turn on the sprinklers, wet*
> *everything, ring the doorbell and book it. Well, he must*
> *have been waiting for us one night because as soon as*
> *we hit the doorbell, he was out of that door in a second.*
> *We scattered. He was a big man. He trapped one of us in*
> *a cul de sac and scared him so bad that we cleaned up*
> *the place and never touched that house again!*
>
> *-Andrew, local*

An Agnes Avenue man reported that on Monday evening he found a male juvenile in his yard. The youth asked to use the phone and the homeowner complied. However, the man said, he held the boy at gunpoint while he used the phone because he was suspicious and fearful of the youth.

LOOKING FOR HOME IN ALL THE WRONG PLACES

It was 2:50 a.m. on Thursday, when Sonoma Police got a call from a resident on Falono Drive complaining that someone was knocking on the front door of his house and trying to get inside. The caller assured police he was not expecting any visitors at that hour, and he added that he could see the intruder through a front window and he seemed to be swaying on his feet. Police responded quickly, but they didn't find anyone knocking on the caller's front door. They did, however, find a 25-year-old man lying on a nearby planter box. When they roused the man and questioned him, he explained he was just trying to go inside the house to get some sleep. When police asked him if it was his house, he said he didn't know. When they asked him where he lived, he said he didn't know that either. At this point, the officers couldn't help noticing the telltale signs of intoxication, including slurred speech, incoherence, bloodshot eyes, a strong odor of alcohol and a propensity to lie down in strange places. At that point the man had what seemed to be a helpful idea. He said he had a friend he could call who knew where he lived and who would be able to come get him.

"Telltale signs of intoxication, including slurred speech, incoherence, bloodshot eyes, a strong odor of alcohol and a propensity to lie down in strange places."

The man then pulled out a cell phone and called his friend. When the friend answered, the man couldn't tell him where he was, so he handed the telephone to the police officer who was privy to that information. When the officer asked the friend on the phone where he was, the friend said he didn't exactly know, and then volunteered that he didn't know or couldn't remember where the man in the planter box lived either. Police concluded that the friend on the phone was probably as drunk as the man in the planter box. With even the most tenuous alternative eliminated, police arrested the planter box man for public intoxication and booked him into the county jail.

A resident of Stoneybrook Drive reported that someone had knocked at his door, and when he answered, he found a white male in his 50s with shoulder length hair, a thin moustache and a cane. The soon-to-be assailant told the resident he was there to collect $150 that was owed to a third party and if the man didn't have the money at that time, it would be $300 next week. When the resident told the cane-carrying assailant he didn't owe anyone any money and didn't know what the man was talking about, the cane-wielder smacked the resident in the mouth with the cane and fled. Deputies contacted the third party to see if she knew the cane-wielding assailant, and she said she didn't know anything about it.

ARMED ROBBER GETS SHORT CHANGED

A 27-year-old man reported Friday afternoon that a former neighbor came over to his apartment on Smith Avenue and demanded money. The man reported that the intruder, described as a 22-year-old white male, pulled out a pocketknife and threatened him with it. When he told the robber that he didn't have any money, the robber turned around, took 20 cents off the television, and said he would be back in two hours for more money. The man did not return. Sheriff's officials say they know who the alleged robber is and have a warrant out for his arrest.

> *There was this regular who would always say, "I want to move back to Virginia, where the people are f%*king normal." She had to be 80 years old. She talked like a sailor.*
>
> *-Kevin, cabbie*

Sometime overnight, someone entered a business on Highway 12, cooked themselves a meal, drank a beer and left leaving the cash register, with $400 in it, untouched.

BE IT EVER SO HUMBLE, THERE'S NO PLACE LIKE (A TOILET) HOME

When a Sonoma police officer investigated a report of someone camping illegally at the Vallejo Home State Historic Park on West Spain Street, at about 7:45 a.m., he wasn't expecting to discover a pair of booted feet sticking out from beneath the door of the plastic portable toilet that stands beside the park's permanent bathroom structure. He was even more **"He wasn't expecting to discover a pair of booted feet sticking out from beneath the door of the plastic portable toilet."** surprised to discover the odor of burning paper drifting out from under the closed door, which has about a 6-inch gap at the bottom. Knocking on the boots didn't produce an appropriate response, so the officer pulled open the door to see what the boots were attached to. Inside he found a 31-year-old transient from Dallas, Texas, who was warming himself by burning newspaper in a metal can. His body, not counting his booted appendages, was prone and occupied most of the five feet of floor space available at the side of the toilet seat. When the officer explained that a fire in a plastic porta-potty was unsafe, the man replied there was nothing to worry about, that, "I do it all the time." The officer then patiently explained that camping in the state park was not allowed and that fires must be confined to approved fire pits, which did not include temporary toilets. The man was cited and released.

BOOK WORM UNEARTHED

A worker at a bed and breakfast on Broadway reported that when she was showing a couple to their room Saturday afternoon, she opened the door and found a man sitting in the corner of the room quietly reading a book. The woman, who had never seen the man before, described him as neat, in his 40's, with long hair in a ponytail. She said he looked up, put down his book, and calmly walked out of the building without saying a word.

THE STRANGE CASE OF THE MYSTERY ENEMA

Even veteran police officers were dumbfounded by a difficult-to-classify act that may or may not have been a crime but which definitely did stretch the boundaries of the bizarre. "You are not," premised a Sonoma Police Sgt., "you are definitely not, going to believe this." The story is brief but no less baffling.

On the afternoon of Sunday, August 9th, a 56-year-old man who is visually impaired - that is to say he could not see well, if at all - was standing in his apartment on Parker Road when a woman appeared in his doorway, unannounced and unexpected. The woman told him she was there to give him an enema. Because the man had recently undergone intestinal surgery, he thought perhaps that explained her presence. The woman deftly guided him to his bedroom, had him drop his pants and lie face down on his bed. She then gave the man an enema and promptly left. The whole episode took about a minute-and-a-half, he later told police. The woman did not leave a card or any other identifying information. And given the condition of his eyesight, the man did not, in the complete sense of the word, actually see her. A day later, on Monday, the enema recipient began wondering about what had happened to him but took no action. By Tuesday, he felt compelled to shed some light on the experience, so he contacted police. An investigating officer promptly called the man's doctor and was told no enema had been prescribed, ordered or approved. Sonoma police turned the case over to the domestic and sexual assault unit of the Sonoma Sheriff's Office who have yet to make sense of the caper. It is well known that fatal enemas have been implicated in conspiracy theories surrounding the deaths of both Napoleon Bonaparte and Marilyn Monroe, but the victim of what may become known in crime annals and police academies across the country as "The Sonoma Enema," apparently reported no ill-effects from the treatment.

DO THESE PANTS MAKE ME LOOK FAT?

I just think it's really funny when people stuff things into their pants.

> *[One] guy shoved a pretty good-sized cheesecake down his pants. I stopped him at the door. He pulled it out of his pants to hand it back to me, but I wasn't going to touch it.*
>
> *-Jacob, store security*

IS THAT A BOTTLE IN YOUR PANTS OR...

Economy-sized booze bottles, sometimes referred to as "jumbos" or "family sized," typically hold 1.75 liters of relatively low grade adult beverage and measure 14 inches in circumference and just over a foot in length. Jumbo bottles do not fit in any conventional pants pocket currently available in clothing stores, but apparently they will fit inside the waistband of some people's trousers. That was the surprising discovery made by an underage young man who was not yet old enough to legally buy alcohol when he walked into the Lucky's Market on Sonoma Highway at 10:30 p.m. on Friday, Aug. 13. Seeming to know just what he wanted, he went straight to the liquor aisle and stuffed a jumbo container of Svedka vodka down the front of his pants. He then headed for the exit, presumably duck-walking as he fled, but was accosted by a loss prevention officer who did not ask the youth if he was happy to see her. When police arrived, the young man was in custody and offered the following explanation: He had been hanging out with friends at a taco truck in the Springs when they decided to drink alcohol. Taking the initiative to solve the supply problem, he said, "I'll be right back." He wasn't.

This guy stuffed some pantyhose down his pants. It was Leggs, in the big egg. He came in walking fine and now he's walking though the store like a cowboy. Awkward.

-Jacob, store security

NUTS IN HIS WAISTBAND

A police officer doing some late-night shopping inside the Sonoma Safeway store, spotted a familiar face and said to the 31-year-old Boyes Hot Springs resident, "Hey, did you forget to go to court?" The sheepish subject of a fail-to-appear warrant answered, "Yes," and the officer promptly conducted a search of his person, which initially turned up five 1.75-ounce bags of Safeway coffee in his pockets. The man explained that he had forgotten he had the coffee and intended to pay for it. A further search revealed two, 6-ounce jars of macadamia nuts in the man's waistband. Asked if he had forgotten them too, the suspect withheld a credible answer.

People get charged with felonies now, especially if there is a plan. One guy had skin-tight tights on underneath his pants. This was so he could stuff bottles of booze in his pants and the tights would hold them there. But he put 4 bottles in there. His legs are twice the size they were, and he's clanking, and he thinks I'm not going to notice it.

-Dan, store security

A man who told a clerk at an El Verano market Wednesday that he was wandering around the store to "compare prices" must not have liked the cost of the schnapps. The clerk reported seeing the man put a bottle of it into his pants and leave without paying.

A Sonoma man was arrested when he was found to have two candy bars in his pocket and a can of chili stuffed down his left sock. The items were stolen from a nearby grocery store.

> *A guy walks into CVS, goes into the liquor aisle and takes two 1.75-liters of booze and puts them in his pockets and tries to walk out of the store. You tell me, how are you going to possibly conceal those huge bottles in your pants? Of course he gets caught because the bottles are hanging out of the top of his pants.*
>
> *-Jim, local*

A shoplifter, who last Wednesday purloined a choice package of steaks from a local supermarket and shoved it down his trousers, didn't reckon that a fellow shopper who witnessed the heist was an alert off-duty police officer. When the suspect stepped outside, a member of a local police department staff identified himself and placed the sirloin swiper under citizen's arrest.

"A shoplifter purloined a choice package of steaks from a local supermarket and shoved it down his trousers."

The suspect was taken into custody, grilled, charged with petty theft and released.

Store security at Lucky Supermarket nabbed two people for shoplifting in three hours. At 3 p.m., a 40-year-old woman was stopped for stealing a 99-cent bunch of carnations, and at 6:15 p.m., a man was stopped leaving without paying for the package of raw shrimp in his pants.

QUACK!

I've jumped my BMX bike over the duck pond. (The narrow part!) I've chased ducks but never caught one. I've fed ducks many times, and I've swam with the ducks. Actually, a friend's dad shoved me in the duck pond when I was a kid. I made a smart-ass comment to him, and he just reached out and pushed me in. Fully clothed. Those ducks have been around a long time.

DUCK TWIRLER DISTURBS PLAZA PASSERBY
A horrified citizen told Sonoma Police Monday that she saw a man in the Plaza twirling a duck around his head and shouting that he was going to have duck for dinner.

Drunken ducks caused quite a flap Monday morning. At 11:00 a.m. police picked up a duck that was "intoxicated and found staggering around the Pyracantha bushes" in the Plaza. They took it to the kennel to dry out. Half an hour later, a city fireman reported having a "dazed and confused" duck in his custody, also found near the Pyracantha bushes. Police suspect the Pyracantha harvest is quite potent this year.

The guy was obviously wasted. It was probably 11 a.m. He came out of the bar, jumped in his truck, thought it was in reverse, gunned it, and there he went. Up over the curb, through the grass and right into the duck pond. He was sitting in his truck, stuck in the duck pond, all jolly drunk, 'til he realized the cops were going to show up.
                                        -Al, Sonoma Parks Employee

Joe Franklin, 26, was arrested for drunkenness after being spotted serenading the ducks in the Plaza duck pond.

One year, they drained the duck pond in the Plaza to clean it, and my bike was at the bottom of it. It had been gone for a while.
                                        -Anderson, local

Someone called police Monday to report a man who just threw his "friend" into the Plaza duck pond.

Before there was a skate park in Sonoma, they drained the duck pond to clean it, and we decided to use it as a skate bowl. The cops weren't too happy about that.
                                        -Sean, local

OWNER JOINS DOG IN DUCK POND SWIM

Police occasionally hear complaints about dogs in the Plaza duck pond. But on Thursday, July 5, they received a report of a dog and its owner swimming in the duck pond together. When police arrived, they found a longtime Sonoma resident standing **"My dog just loves ducks."** at the edge of the pond soaked to the skin while his black lab continued to romp happily in the pond. The triple-digit temperatures notwithstanding, the dog's owner said he knew he and his dog weren't supposed to be in the pond and that the dog should have been on a leash. But he expressed ignorance of the long-standing law prohibiting dogs in the Plaza at all and added, "My dog just loves ducks." The officer pointed out that there were no ducks in the pond and that the presence of the man's dog might be one of the reasons. Ignorance of the no-dogs Plaza policy may be more widespread than city authorities realize because signs prohibiting dogs are not widely distributed. Police said the man was cooperative, although, as one officer later observed, "Common sense would dictate that you should not bring a duck-hunting dog to a duck pond." The man was cited and released.

> *Sometimes when it was a really slow day, we would catch a duck in the Plaza, bring it over to the car and turn on the mic. The duck would start honking, "Quack! Quack!" And that would go over the airwaves to the station and other officers.*
>
> *-Officer Thomas, Sonoma Police*

Someone called police to say a duck with a Plaza Park address had a plastic ring around its neck. He appeared to be fine after officers checked him out to make sure he was ok.

> *I was pretty drunk, and I came out of Gino's at the time and there was a duck on my jeep. I was so pissed off I chased the duck into the park and was chasing it around and around. Eventually, I gave up and I drove home. Well, 25 minutes later, an Officer Jenkins shows up at my house and tells me he* **"He says he's got to write me a ticket because people saw me chasing a duck around in the park."** *has to write me ticket because people saw me chasing a duck around in the park. I knew the officer and I said, "O.K., do what you need to." I go to court, and the Judge*

says I have to help clean the park for a year. That's my punishment. Then the prosecutor says, "Hold on." And he walks up to the judge and whispers in his ear. And the judge says, "You've got to teach boxing at the Boy's Club for a year." So I taught boxing at the Boy's Club for a year.
Ted, local

LAY DOWN THE BOTTLE

The summer after high school, I worked at Sears Point Raceway (now Sonoma Raceway). A few friends and I would do maintenance during the week and security on the weekends. By "maintenance," I mean pick up trash on the property that was left from the 80,000 visitors the previous weekend. But the payoff was on the weekend. We were in charge of scouring the crowds in the stands and collecting beer from them if they had brought their own. Usually it went down like this. Me: "Sir, your going to have to give me your beer." Longhaired, bearded guy wearing a leather vest who could kill me with one punch: "Hell if I'm giving you my beer, kid, beat it!" Me: "Sir, I can have the police up here in 3 minutes, and you will be removed from the raceway, possibly charged, and put on a list for future races." Longhaired, bearded guy wearing a leather vest who could kill me in one punch: "This is bulls#%t! Fine. Here." He hands me the beer he was drinking. Me: "I'm going to need the full 6 pack, sir." This would happen multiple times a day. So by the time we were heading home from work, we would have a case or two of beer and head back to Sonoma to party with our friends. People like to party in Sonoma. Sometimes the cops are there, and sometimes they're not.

Deputies found a man, his face painted black with shaving cream on his head, in an allegedly intoxicated state on Highway 12, Sunday afternoon. Tom Calhoun told officers he was the victim of a "party prank."

> *He used to hitchhike in Glen Ellen. He would get so drunk, but he was a friendly drunk. He'd start out standing up, but if no one picked him up, he would lie down on the ground on the side of the road with his arm up and his thumb out. He would be almost passed out but had enough energy to keep that arm up. One time we picked him up, and my mom and dad had to lift him into the car.*
>
> *-Seth, local*

WOMAN CAN'T NAME MAN WITH HEAD IN HER SHIRT

It was still 15 minutes before noon, when a Sonoma police officer, parked across the street from the Blue Moon Saloon, watched a couple come staggering out the door, the woman noticeably unsteady on her feet. Impaired as she appeared to be, the woman nevertheless began dancing provocatively in front of her companion and was soon raising and lowering her shirt in what looked to the officer like a simulated striptease.

Taking the act a significant step further, the woman then lifted her shirt over the man's head, trapping his

"Was soon raising and lowering her shirt in what looked to the officer like a simulated striptease."

face against her chest as he began wagging his head back and forth. Having witnessed more than enough of the very public display, the officer drove across the street and into the saloon's parking lot, the happy couple oblivious to his arrival. It was not until the officer exited the car and slammed the door that his presence was noted and the man retrieved his head from the woman's shirt.

When the officer inquired as to just what they were doing, the woman happily explained that she was showing the man the decorative metal rings she had recently had attached to sensitive parts of her anatomy.

She readily offered her name and when the officer asked how long she had been drinking she explained she had "been partying since 9 p.m." the previous night. When the officer asked the man his name, he mumbled something incomprehensible, addled perhaps by alcohol and his recent immersion in the woman's shirt. He also seemed to lack any significant familiarity with the English language.

The officer therefore turned back to the merry dancer and asked her for the man's name, to which she blithely admitted, "I have absolutely no idea."

> *If you go to Woodstock, you're going to get a tie-dyed t-shirt and listen to music. If you go to Sonoma what are you going to do? Drink.*
>
> *-Barry, local*

Two allegedly intoxicated men, found sitting on the front porch of an El Verano bar, were ordered by deputies to pick up the beer cans that were lying around. They reportedly had trouble standing but managed to get the job done and were off. A short time later, officers found one standing in the middle of Verano Avenue, with his pants down around his ankles. The other was spotted falling down the edge of the road on Riverside Drive.

"Officers found one standing in the middle of Verano Avenue, with his pants down around his ankles."

They were rounded up and taken to county jail.

A woman in a purple robe was spotted staggering down Arnold drive at 7:30 p.m. Wednesday.

> *People say, "Oh your from Sonoma, you must know about wine," and I'd say, "I drink the cheap stuff," which is true.*
>
> *-Amy, local*

An officer spotted a man at 3:50 a.m. the same morning. He was standing shirtless in the back yard of a business on First Street West. The man was reportedly yelling, "Let me in. Let me in" at a window. The officer determined that the man was heavily intoxicated at this point and "was arguing with his reflection in the window." The man was arrested on suspicion of public intoxication and taken to county jail.

> *Teen Safe Ride was a company of volunteers that would pick kids up and take them home for free if you needed a ride. John had to have used Teen Safe Ride until he was 20 or 21. It was cheaper than a cab.*
>
> *-Robert, local*

BOYES MAN GETS TAKEN FOR A RIDE

A night of beer guzzling and a cruise on the rear of a stranger's motorcycle landed a Boyes Hot Springs man in Sonoma Valley Hospital early Sunday following a strange series of events that deputies are still attempting to piece together. Officers were called to the hospital early Sunday where they interviewed the 21-year-old man who told them in detail about his wild, if not unbelievable, night. The man said the previous night he had been partying at Lovall Valley Circle, and after downing a case and a half of beer, he headed toward Sonoma, when a blond cyclist stopped to give him a ride. At a sharp curve in the road, the cyclist wiped out, dumping his bike and passenger on the ground. The hitchhiking beer drinker said he awoke several hours later lying in some roadside shrubbery, not only were the cyclist and his motorcycle gone, but so was the man's wallet

"The hitchhiking beer drinker said he awoke several hours later lying in some roadside shrubbery."

containing $130. The cyclist did, however, leave him the remainder of a 12-pack of beer, which the injured man said he downed before walking to the local hospital. Deputies said they could find no evidence of an accident on Lovall Valley Road nor could they find any scrapes or bruises on the man.

In the Eighties, there were 10 county bars in a 2-mile radius and 2 guys on shift to deal with it. Three Nations. The London Lodge. Denny's Club. Mr. Roberts. Uncle Patty's. Creekside Café. The Roadhouse. McNeely's. Inskeeps. The Bonanza Club. That's not including any of the bars on the Square.

-Officer Jenkins, Sonoma Police

At 3 a.m. Sunday, deputies were called to Groom Street on the report of a guy wedged between the bridge and a fence. He was liberated and taken to Sonoma Valley Hospital. Officers said that booze helped the guy get into his predicament.

I used to like the wine with no grapes, called Thunderbird! I don't drink anymore.

-Gordon, cabbie

LOCAL FREQUENT FLYER CREDITED WITH 'GRAND SLAM'

Some Sonoma police officers have referred to it as a "grand slam," baseball parlance for scoring four runs by hitting a bases-loaded homer. The honor goes to a Sonoma transient with an appetite for alcohol and a penchant for landing in police custody when he drinks. That happened four times between April 22 and April 28, a record even some of Sonoma's veteran "frequent flyers" would have trouble matching.

Her husband comes to pick her up in his car, and he's as drunk as she is.

-Officer Hamil, Sonoma Security

Deputies found a drunk man in front of his dad's home Thursday evening. He told them that he wanted to go to an alcohol rehabilitation center in Santa Rosa. Officers obliged and started driving the 33-year-old man north. Sometime while in route, he changed his mind, so officers were compelled to drop him off at jail.

He was jumping on car hoods, strutting around, takes his shirt off, everyone is yelling at him to go home. Then he goes to his car and starts revving his car and doing 360's in front of the Swiss Hotel. Unbelievable.

-Marie, local

Deputies spotted a drunken, drooling man staggering down the middle of the road.

We used to take guys home that were drunk. Not anymore. What if they burned the house down? It's about responsibility now.

-Officer Flynn, Sonoma Police

There was a group of us. We started out wine tasting in the morning. We hit about 5 or 7 wineries. We were very loaded. We got back in the afternoon and decided to go for a swim. I didn't have a swimsuit, so I went swimming in my underwear. Afterwards, I put my pants back on, but I went commando, because my underwear were still wet. I got in an argument with this guy, and then I decide I'll leave the place. I walk outside, and I realize I have no idea where I am. So, I decide I'll just sit down on the curb and wait for a minute. It's around 3 in the afternoon. Well, that cement felt pretty darn good, and I was pretty drunk, so I decided to rest up. I guess I fell asleep on the sidewalk. I'm then awakened by a Sonoma Police officer. He decided to cuff me, while I had a pair of wet underwear in my hands. He obviously asked me about the underwear, and I told him I had gone swimming earli-

"He decided to cuff me, while I had a pair of wet underwear in my hand."

er, just inside the condo. He told me, he was going to take me in to the station, and I can sleep it off in the cell but that he wouldn't ticket me. So I get put in the drunk tank,

I sleep it off for a couple of hours. Get out around 7:30, walk down to the Square and find my friends at a bar and continue drinking. I really didn't think much of it, until a couple of days later when I come into the restaurant I was working at, in Sonoma, and one of my co-workers had cut out the police report, and there it was. It said that I was found on a sidewalk, passed out, IN my underwear. They had my name in the report. I was re-

"They had my name in the report. I was really embarressed because everyone saw it."

ally embarrassed because everyone saw it: co-workers, manager, friends. Then a couple of nights later this local girl that we went to high school with comes into the restaurant. She asks my buddy, who I work with, if I'm okay. He tells her, "Yeah, he's fine, why?" She said, "Because I heard that he was found naked, passed out, in a ditch." So I went from having underwear in my hand, to being IN my underwear on the sidewalk, to being naked, passed out, in a ditch. All in a few days.

-Greg, from Napa

A man, 23, of Napa was arrested on suspicion of public intoxication after he was found sleeping in his underwear on a Blue Wing Drive sidewalk.

I came here from other parts of the country. At some point, wine became a staple: a food group. It's hard to go to an event, any social event in Sonoma where they don't have wine being served. And that has to influence people's behavior to a certain extent.

-Jim, local

A deputy responded to a report of a man down at the Broadway Market and found the man in a fetal position behind a bush. The man was reportedly unable to stand or walk on his own and said that he was celebrating his birthday.

> *Mimosas and Bloody Marys starting at 8 a.m. before the parade. Tradition.*
> -Beth, local

A 55-year-old transient man was booked into county jail for an outstanding misdemeanor warrant and being publicly intoxicated. While enroute to the jail, the man reportedly urged officers to hurry because he had consumed two 40-ounce bottles of beer.

> *Up in Lovell Valley loop there was a big still in a barn. We went up there as kids, and it was quite large. Lots of cans on the walls that had shotgun holes through them. The Feds had come in and shot the whole place up during prohibition. They got caught because there were all of these huge trucks taking sugar up there. They were trying to make it look like a dairy, but the Feds caught them.*
> -Tom, local

BAD HAIR, SEXY HAIR

An officer on foot patrol along the east side of the Plaza saw a well-known transient stumbling along with a staggered gait, looking disheveled. As the officer approached, the shaky man addressed him by name and said in a belligerent voice, "What do you want?" Knowing the man was on searchable probation with a requirement that he not consume or possess alcohol, the officer questioned him, he became argumentative, agitated and acknowledged only that he had downed "two tall boys." The officer took the man into custody and tried to place him in the squad car, but he kept refusing to put his legs inside the vehicle, at one point criticizing the officer's haircut and informing him, "My hair looks sexy," and, "If I saw you out of uniform, I'd kick your ass."

This guy blew like a .367 or a .372 alcohol, and he was proud of it. He should have been dead, drinking that much.

-Jim, local

There was a period of time there, where we had so many locals that were getting busted all of the time cause they were drunk. We literally had their booking sheets pre-made out. We'd spend some extra time just sitting there having a cup of coffee and filling out their names and everything including the charge of being drunk in public. So that when we arrested them, the paperwork only took us a quarter of the time it would have.

-Officer Jenkins, Sonoma Police

COPS RAIN ON MAN'S PARADE

A 22-year-old man who was drinking and playing horseshoes with his friends in Depot Park was arrested for urinating in public Friday afternoon. Officers reported that the park was crowded with families and children at the time the man decided to urinate in their midst. The man called additional attention to himself by urinating in wide sweeping arcs while yelling at his friends to watch him.

This woman got in the cab and projectile vomited from the backseat to the front. Calamari, Chardonnay, and Feta Cheese. That was one of the worst.

-Gordon, cabbie

Police responded to an alarm at the Exchange Bank on West Napa Street when an inebriated customer caused a disturbance while trying to change a Jamaican $100 bill. The bank explained that it does not convert foreign currency for people who don't have accounts, but the man refused to leave and became increasingly irate, apparently expecting to convert the sizable Jamaican bill into some useful U.S. currency. Had the man been less intoxicated and more familiar with currency exchange rates, he might not have bothered. At the current rate of exchange, a Jamaican dollar is worth 1.389 U.S. cents, so the bill he was desperately trying to convert was worth $1.38. That's not nearly enough for a 40-ounce beer, but more than enough to land the 52-year-old resident of Trail, Ore. in jail on a charge of public intoxication.

> **"So the bill he was trying to convert was worth $1.38. That's not nearily enough for a 40-ounce beer."**

> *You have a real genuine funny and sad, alcoholic sub-culture of all classes: frequent fliers to completely functioning alcoholics.*
>
> *-Jim, local*

NOT A GIANTS' PROSPECT

A 26-year-old transient exited the Town Square bar with a pint glass and threw it at a group of people assembled across the street. The man's aim was mercifully poor and the glass shattered harmlessly without hurting anyone. When a police officer arrived, the man took refuge back inside the bar, and hid in the men's room where he tried to take off the black hoodie sweatshirt he was wearing, presumably to change his appearance. But the officer found him in the bathroom, highly intoxicated and, after a brief resistance, placed the man in handcuffs and under arrest. Asked why he threw the glass at the group of people, the man explained, "I was just throwing a drink to my friend and he missed."

> *The Irish Biking team was in town for the big Coors bike race. A few of locals took the team out to the bars on the Plaza and got them completely drunk the night before the race. They performed so poorly the next day that the following year the people who run the team wouldn't allow the bikers to stay in the town of Sonoma.*
>
> *-Timothy, local*

MY CAR IS IN THE SHOP

I had an idea to start a rickshaw business in Sonoma when I was 15. I ended up washing dishes at Mary's Pizza Shack and being a busser at the Swiss Hotel instead. Here are some other unique modes of transit used in Sonoma.

BALLOON MAKES ILLEGAL LANDING
To the delight of nearby children, a hot air balloon made a surprise landing in a residential area of El Verano Tuesday morning. Sheriff's deputies were dispatched to Railroad Ave. shortly after 8:30 a.m. on a report of a hot air passenger balloon, which had descended in the area. Upon locating the balloon at the end of School Street the pilot reportedly told officers he had been aiming to land in the El Verano elementary school yard, but missed.

We had way too many drinks on the Square, and we were walking back to my place through the Plaza. We see this shopping cart in front of City Hall. So I jump in it, and Jimmy pushes me as fast as he can down East Napa Street. Well, before we know it, a cop rolls up on us, throws on the lights and tells us to pull over using the speaker on the cop car. While the cops are questioning us, pissed that we were drinking and messing around

with the shopping cart, a taxicab pulls up and tells the
cops that they will take us home, which was totally cool.
We didn't really think anything about it, until it made the
headlines of the police report a few days later, "COPS
HALT SHOPPING CART RIDE."

-Otis, local

COPS HALT GROCERY CART RIDE

After receiving a call about a traffic hazard in the wee hours of the morning Wednesday, officers met up with a man pushing another man in a shopping cart down the middle of East Napa Street near First Street East. The cart was confiscated and the two were sent home in a cab.

LAWN-MOWER DRIVER NABBED FOR DUI

An apparently intoxicated Kenwood man found out that even though he was only driving his lawn tractor, he can still get arrested for driving under the influence. On Saturday, Oct. 2, at approximately 7:50 p.m., California Highway Patrol Officer Paul Kelter was on routine patrol in the Kenwood area, when he saw a male driving a lawn mower through the parking lot of the Kenwood Market. The driver exited the lot and proceeded south on Green Street. The lawn mower did not have any lights and was difficult to see. The officer pulled in behind the mower and made a traffic stop. While speaking to the driver, the officer noted the odor of an alcoholic beverage emitting from the 55-year-old man's breath. The driver told the officer that he occasionally uses the mower to drive to the store and get groceries. The officer observed further signs of intoxication, and initiated a DUI investigation. Kelter determined that the man was under the influence and arrested him. The man was booked into the Sonoma County Jail. The unlicensed would-be motorist has two prior DUIs. He told the officer that the mower and his bike were his primary modes of transportation.

There was a guy from the Schellville area that lived out there for a number of years. I don't know if he lived on his own, but he had a horse and he used to ride his horse in and tie his horse behind Steiners. And I guess ride his horse home when the bar closed.

-Officer Reed, Sonoma Police

BICYCLE TRANSFORMED. DIVINE INTERVENTION?

A devout worshipper attending morning Mass at St. Francis Solano Church on Wednesday emerged from the service at 9:15 a.m. to retrieve the bicycle he had left leaning against the building. The bike, his usual means of transport, was a Schwinn single-speed, girl's mountain bike, silver in color with green highlights and black baskets front and back. But it wasn't there. Perhaps puzzled that someone would violate the sanctity of the Lord's house, the man then noticed a different bicycle lying next to the spot where his bike had been. This one was a 10-speed, Free Spirit Canyon Pass, a bike made by Sears up through at least the 1970s. The police report reveals no sign of divine intervention, no indication that a minor miracle had transformed the single-speed into a 10-speed, no evidence at all, in fact, to suggest where the first bike went or the second one came from. Being a law-abiding citizen, the man made no assumptions about the 10-speed's ownership and, after no one showed up to claim it, he took it to the Sonoma Police Department, where it remains, awaiting its owner. Police promise to report if the bike is further transformed into a specialized titanium, 21-speed Stump Jumper with the disc brakes and the Shimano XTR derailleur.

I had a couple of bicycles that I was going to get rid of. Well, Gary Connelly, a fellow officer, his son was redoing bikes. He'd get them at the police auction and stuff like that and use different parts and whatever to rebuild bikes. So I told

"Oh my gosh... here's the coroner's wagon in my driveway!!"

him to swing by and pick up a couple of bikes that I had. The kids didn't use them anymore, and they were broken and that kind of stuff. So, I hear a car in the driveway one day and look out. Oh my gosh... here's the coroner's wagon in my driveway!! Well, this officer was on duty that morning, so he pulled through the driveway to pick up the bicycles for his son, and he was in the coroner's wagon. We loaded the wagon up and off he went.

-Officer Reed, Sonoma Police

A hot air balloon owner may be in hot water with authorities. The report alleges the owner landed his balloon Saturday on a public sidewalk in El Verano in order to pick up passengers and fuel.

An elderly man, described as "disoriented, intoxicated, and belligerent" by deputies, was treated by Schell Vista fire fighters for minor injuries after he traveled three blocks on Napa Road in his electric wheelchair.

Walter McCracken, superintendent of grounds at Sonoma National Golf Course, reported June 25 that persons broke into a shed housing golf carts on the course, took 11 carts out and played bumper cars with them, crashing into several trees.

Deputies were sent to the 15000 block of Highway 12 after receiving a report that an intoxicated woman was seen crawling along the road. When they arrived, sure enough, they found the 68-year-old Boyes Hot Springs resident navigating the roadway on her hands and knees. The crawler was arrested on a charge of public intoxication.

I had to back a trailer/tractor with the Sonoma Home-
town band on it around the square. I was told that I was
a few inches away from running over a little old lady in a
chair watching the parade. Boy, that would have sucked.

-Henry, local

A 41-year-old man who had fallen off his bicycle was arrested for public intoxication. At first, the man blamed his misfortune on the lack of a bicycle path, but then admitted that he had been drinking wine all day long. When asked why, he responded, "Because this is the wine country."

There was a drunk local, young guy, and the cops were
tired of dealing with him. So, the story was that they
drove him up to the top of Mt. Tamalpias and dropped
him off and took his shoes. And by the time the cops got
back to Sonoma the guy had already hitched a ride and
beat them back to the Plaza.

-Amy, local

A unicycle was found on the roof of a building at 165 W. Napa Street.

SHUT IT!

Sonoma is a beautiful, peaceful town. For the most part, it is pretty quiet, unless there is a fire somewhere. That's when they will blow the giant siren out at Schell-Vista to alert the volunteer firefighters to come help. You can hear it through the valley. That's an acceptable noise at anytime. Here are some less acceptable sounds.

COPS RESPOND TO 'GROWLER'

Several reports of incessant "growling" on the Sonoma bike path were received by police in the wee hours Tuesday. Twice, police discovered it was only a man chowing down loudly. Just before 1 a.m. a resident of Enriquez Drive complained that a suspicious person, hanging out near her residence, was yelling and growling. Police were unable to find the growler. About an hour later, officers received a similar complaint of a man emitting "gasping and vomiting noises" on the bike path. This time they found a man "enjoying a snack." "He just makes a lot of noise when he eats," police said. Thirty minutes later, the muncher was still bugging neighbors, this time in the area of Junipero Serra Drive. He was still working on the same snack and police told him to move along.

A Boyes Springs resident was apparently disturbing neighbors at 3 a.m. Wednesday night with his loud "pre-Super bowl victory party." He was apparently celebrating alone and was asked to lower the music.

A South Broadway resident called police Thursday evening to complain about loud rock and roll music coming from a nearby church. Officers following up, found the choir practicing the usual church music. No "Twisted Sister" to be found.

> *When we were bored, we'd go out to the airfield in Schell-ville, (this was when it was flat, not raised runways) and chase rabbits with our patrol cars at night, spinning doughnuts and chasing them. Pretty soon we'd get a call that there are kids spinning doughnuts and making a lot of noise. Well, we told them we'd take care of it immediately. It was us the whole time.*
>
> *-Officer Thomas, Sonoma Police*

Participants in a loud, hot tub party on Connell Court were contacted by police around 2:40 a.m. Saturday and asked to cool it.

A caller complained that a Plymouth Road man was "praying too loud" on Wednesday.

Obnoxious flute music was irritating the residents of Greene Street late Monday. Police were unable to hear the flute.

The radio in a car parked on Second Street West for two days was on. Police turned it off Wednesday.

A Chase Street resident called the City Hall on Monday to complain about the ice cream vendors chimes being too loud as he made his rounds between 7:30 and 8:00 p.m. The vendor was notified.

A father and son playing badminton on Apple Tree Court at 2:39 a.m. Saturday got the attention of neighbors who called the police. After a second complaint and a second visit by officers, the duo agreed to go inside and continue their game at a more reasonable hour.

BIG BOOOM CREATES A BIG STINK

Sonoma Police received numerous calls from eastside residents who were startled by a loud noise at 2 a.m. Sunday. The big boom came from the area of Second Street East and East Spain Street. Investigating officers found that a garlic bucket exploded.

Police received reports that "horrible noises" were coming from the Plaza amphitheater Tuesday afternoon. It turned out to be an impromptu rock concert, which was closed down due to a lack of a permit.

DAYLIGHT DOESN'T DISSUADE "WEREWOLF OF LARSON PARK"

Sheriff's deputies don't know whether it was something the man ate, something he drank or maybe something he smoked. Whatever it was, a 24-year-old Boyes Hot Springs resident was discovered growling and barking in and around the area of Larson Park, in broad daylight, without the benefit of a full moon. It all started at about 8:10 a.m., when a man who was playing soccer at Larson Park went to use one of the portable toilets. He opened a toilet door only to find a fully-dressed man **"A man was growling** inside the stall. The soccer player **and barking at him."** closed the door and walked back to his game but before long, the man in the portable potty came out with his fists clenched, his body rigid - and he was growling. The portable potty man then started chasing the soccer player around the tennis courts, eventually catching up with him and pushing him to the ground. During the fall, the soccer player lost some belongings from his pocket, items his pursuer scooped up and then left the park. When deputies from the Sheriff 's Office responded, they took a report and, from past experience, had a good idea who they were looking for. A second call soon came in from a person on Byrd Avenue who reported a man was growling and barking at him there. Deputies quickly located the growler and attempted to place him under arrest, but he became combative before eventually being cuffed and placed in the squad car. The growling man was charged with felony robbery and resisting arrest. He was booked into the county jail but there was no indication in the police report whether or not his cell came with a fire hydrant.

Woodside Lane residents complained at 11 p.m. Sunday that neighborhood cows are moooooooooooooing too loudly. The cows' owner was contacted, but he's unsure what he's going to do about the boisterous bovines.

A dog, who lives on Siesta Way, was mouthing off Saturday night. He was told to muzzle it.

A resident of Patten Street called police just after 5:30 a.m. Saturday after hearing someone sneeze in front of her house. Officers suspect the sneezer was a cat.

Worried residents of East Napa Street called police Saturday to report hearing a shotgun blast. Investigating officers said it wasn't a gun they heard but rather an errant duck who had flown into the power lines, triggering an explosion. The flight wasn't fatal for the duck, who was taken to the police department kennel to recover.

A resident of West Spain Street complained Tuesday evening that she heard growling. It turned out to be frogs.

VEHICLE FUN BACKFIRES

A pickup truck driver causing his vehicle to make backfiring noises resulted in a high-risk traffic stop Friday, as police suspected gunfire. Starting at approximately 10 a.m., Sonoma Valley residents were reporting to the **"They were hearing gunshots in various locations throughout the Valley."** police that they were hearing gunshots in various locations throughout the Valley. The reports subsided until shortly after 8:30 p.m., when more calls were being made to report additional gunshots. The witnesses also reported seeing a white pickup truck driving south on Arnold Drive in Glen Ellen. Witnesses believed this truck was responsible for the gunshots. The Chief of the Sonoma Police Department had just left a community gathering in the Boyes Hot Springs area and was driving south on Highway 12 near Maxwell Village Shopping Center when he saw a white pickup truck also southbound. He then heard several loud bangs and could see flashes consistent with gunfire coming from the truck. Officers from the Sonoma Police Department and the Sonoma County Sheriff's Department converged on the area, and the suspect vehicle was stopped at Seventh Street and Napa Street.

Based on the potential for a weapon to be in the car, Napa Street was closed to vehicle traffic. The driver and the three occupants were removed from the vehicle at gunpoint. The vehicle was searched, but no weapons were found.

The driver admitted to the officers that he had deliberately caused his vehicle to make backfire sounds and had been doing so all day. The driver was released with a stern admonishment concerning his behavior.

An over-zealous leaf-blower was told to knock it off for a while at 4:44 a.m. at Maxwell Village Shopping Center Saturday.

In an act that could qualify for consideration by the Darwin Awards committee, an unlicensed driver went to unusual lengths to draw attention to herself on May 8. State law limits the level of sound that can be heard from the stereo system of a vehicle. If you can hear Geto Boys or 50 Cent beyond

"If you can hear Geto Boys or 50 Cent beyond 50 feet, it's too loud."

50 feet, it's too loud. That's a section of the vehicle code the driver of a blue 1999 Nissan Altima apparently wasn't familiar with when she blasted the car's stereo system in front of Sonoma Valley High School. The sound was more than loud enough to reach the ears of the school's safety officer who made a traffic stop at 8:15 a.m. to quiet the racket. That was when he discovered the driver had no license, and that may have been when it dawned on the driver that making use of a mega-watt stereo system when you can't legally drive the car in which the system is installed is several steps short of brilliant. The driver was cited for having a "loud outside vehicle amplification system" and, of course, driving without a license.

YEEHAH DUDE!!
Police were alerted to a disturbance in Depot Park after a citizen called to report that someone was shouting "yeeehah," in the vicinity. A police officer responded on foot and, sure enough, heard the distinct screech of someone shouting, "yeeehah," coming from the Casa Grande parking lot at the edge of the park. Advancing under cover of darkness, the officer saw a 36-year-old Sonoma man riding a bicycle around and around the parking lot and shouting, "yeeehah." After seeing enough to assess the situation with a reasonable degree of understanding, the officer stepped out of the darkness, shone his flashlight at the yeeehahing cyclist and ordered him to stop.
The yeeehah-er continued his vocally enhanced pedaling, showing no inclination to stop, so the officer reached out, pulled him off the bike and speedily handcuffed him.

U.F.O.'s, GHOSTS, AND WEIRD STUFF

There was a haunted house on 4th Street East and I remember people talking about a lady dressed all in white with white hair appearing near the cemetery at dusk. I swear I saw her once. Whether real or not, it freaked me out. I can't say I've seen any U.F.Os, but I've seen plenty of weird things in the Valley of the Moon.

Two prosthetic feet were found in a parking lot of a business in the 1000 block of Napa Road Monday morning.

I heard one of the brothers ate a cow patty and died.
-Amy, local

Deputies reported sighting a giant light bulb late Saturday night on the east edge of Sonoma, but it turned out to be the huge hot air balloon that was part of the 130th Anniversary celebration at Buena Vista Winery.

A Schellville woman reported finding a large, decapitated animal carcass on her lawn, which she thought might be connected to some sort of cult ritual.

There are a lot of strange things here. Sonoma Valley is one of the most haunted places around. There is something going on out here. I'd go up to Buena Vista numerous times and a door would open right in front of me. Nobody around, nothing. I'd pull my gun, but there was nothing there. How can 150-year-old huge doors, just open themselves? It freaked me the heck out.

-Officer Hamil, Sonoma Security

A man dressed in black and clutching a fired-up chain saw jumped in front of a car on West Spain Street just after midnight Friday. The female driver said it appeared the chain saw was on.

This guy asked me to take him to the US Bank in Santa Rosa. So, he made me park down the alleyway from the bank. He was disheveled and acting weird and I thought he was going to rob the bank, because he comes out with all this money. Bundles of cash in his duffle bag and hands and money coming out of his pockets, and I'm like "Oh my god, I'm the getaway car." He said it was $30,000. He looked like the **"Oh my god, I'm the getaway car."** *biggest bum. Teeth missing, smelly, had a beat up guitar with cobwebs on it. So, we head back to Sonoma, and he was threatening to throw the money out the window, telling me "money is the root of all evil." Acting so weird. I saw a helicopter. Freaked out. He started asking me about my kids and then started giving me hundreds and hundreds. I made $1,000 on that one ride. He was in Sonoma for the weekend. He lived in Berkeley. I took him back home at the end of the weekend and everyone on the block knew him. I made $1,000 on that one ride.*

-Ellen, cabbie

A woman who came home with a guy from a nightclub early Saturday to his Vineburg residence called deputies to ask for a ride home. The woman told deputies that she became concerned when the guy and his sister started fighting over "who gets her."

Glen Ellen sky watchers called officers early Tuesday to report a sighting of an unidentified flying object. White and green lights were flashing in the area of Jack London State Park, the caller said. Deputies checked it out and found nothing flashing.

> *This town at night has a strange horror about it. I know a lot of people don't believe in ghosts, and I didn't until I started working nights in Sonoma.*
> *-Officer Hamil, Sonoma Security*

A Sonoma woman reported late Saturday that she saw "funny lights" in the sky- first two, then three. They were "brighter than the stars and fascinating."

> *I was new to the job and it was the first time I picked her up. She wouldn't get in the cab until I drank Holy Water. I had to do whatever I could to get her in the car because we were so backed up. The boss was yelling on the radio and had a lot of people waiting for cabs... so I just knocked it back, drank it and she got in... the other cabbie didn't have to do that because he was a Catholic.*
> *-Ellen, cabbie*

"She wouldn't get in the cab until I drank Holy Water."

A man's leg was seen hanging out of the trunk of a tan Honda automobile on East Napa Street at 7 a.m. Monday, according to a woman who saw the same. Police were unable to locate the leg or the car.

An 18th century painting of the crucifixion stolen from the Sonoma mission in 1979 was returned this week. Valued at $12,500, the painting was reportedly found under an abandoned house in Vineberg by a man hunting for old bottles. It was in good condition.

> *We find lots of shoes. How can people leave shoes in a cab? How can you jump out of the cab and not realize you don't have a shoe or both of your shoes on?*
> *-Kevin, cabbie*

A woman called police at 10:53 p.m. Wednesday to report a man sitting inside Great Western Bank. Investigating officers found that the man was a dedicated employee working late.

Two women reported a set of suspicious circumstances. The women told police that a strange man they had seen at the library was later seen by them at Albertsons.

> *You have no idea what kind of calls we would get! Oh my God. There was a woman living on Twinn St. and I know one officer went out there several times. He's now dead, but I can remember Derek Vincent went out to the same woman a number of times that I was working, and the woman would report... aliens. She didn't call them aliens, but the lights were getting to her and, "it's from the spaceship." It was aliens. And the flashing lights, and they are landing in her back yard. This went on and on and on, and*

"It's from the spaceship. It was aliens. And the flashing light, and they are landing in her back yard."

I know this one time Derek came in and he told her to put foil on her head and that would repel the aliens. He said, "I was nice, I just told her that you know, what I've heard, is that if you cover your windows with foil, that blocks the rays and the light." And she did. She also reported that the little things were up there above the cabinet, and I think one time she was complaining because the aliens were putting black spots in the grout above her bathtub. Another time, she thought that they had taken her silverware. She knew it was those little people that come around.

-Officer Reed, Sonoma Police

A $1 bill was found in the lobby of the Sonoma Police Department.

Newlyweds found $13,000 of jewelry they had reported stolen from their room at an inn in Sonoma on Oct. 31. They told officers that they found the jewelry in a makeup bag in their luggage when they got home.

Becky Todd, the police officer, and I meet up at Vallejo's home. She looks up at the window in the house, around 1 in the morning, and there was a woman in a dress standing at the window. We both saw it. Then the curtain shut and that was that. I also saw a man in this building up at Hanna. Clear as day, through the window. Alarm on the building, and he's looking at me and I'm looking at him. All the doors were locked. Hanna is one of the most haunted places in this town.

-Officer Hamil, Sonoma Security

A white tombstone found on Petaluma Avenue was turned into police.

I was out on Eighth Street. I see this giant thing in the sky. Looked like a UFO. It's me and two other officers. It looked like a giant light in the sky. It was dry cleaner plastic bags with a flame in them flying through the sky. I got teased for a month after that.

-Officer Hamil, Sonoma Security

SPACE ALIENS IN MOBILE HOME PARK?

Police aren't sure whether it was a case of malicious vandalism, a work of impromptu outdoor art or the result of space aliens. But a mobile home resident on Fairview Drive told police that sometime between midnight and 3 a.m., a line of plants was moved outside her residence, a bag of Miracle-Gro plant food was emptied in a line on her driveway, two large pots were placed on her car, a garbage can was placed on top of her carport, a basket was put on the roof of her home and garden tools and a hose were arranged in her trees.

ACKNOWLEDGEMENTS

First and foremost I want to thank The Sonoma Index-Tribune, David Bolling and Bill Lynch for their encouragement and for allowing me to sift through 30 years of police reports and use them for this book. Thanks David for your great sense of humor and thank you to the different writers who, over the years, have written some very funny reports for the newspaper. Many thanks to the retired law enforcement officers from the Sonoma Police Department and the Sonoma Valley Sheriff's department who shared their experiences with me. So much thanks to all of the locals, and you know who you are, who shared your funny stories about Sonoma!

Thanks to Biff Barnes for copy-editing.

Thanks, for many and varied reasons to: John Billingsley, Bonnie Friedericy, Gary Twinn, Amy Segal Burke, Terry Scannell, Dan Murphy, Jennifer Gray, Davis Campbell, Tony Essa, Mary Louise Brumit, Adam Byrd, the crew at TDA, Daedalus Howell, everyone at Capo and the Blue Shirts, and the Sonomans who read early editions and gave me notes.

Thank you to my family. Thanks to Joe Herrschaft, Douglas Thompson, Jeff Cuda, peeps at The Swiss and the Town Square for listening to me ramble on about reports and stories to see if they were actually funny to someone other than myself.

The most thanks is for my wife, Kirsten, who has cheered me on all the way through this and offered amazing guidance and ideas that have shaped this book. I'm very grateful for your love, quick wit, honesty and the fact that you can make me fall over with laughter.

AUTHORS NOTE

All names have been changed in this book. Names of suspects, officers and locals, have been changed to protect their identity. In some cases, I have used a couple different names for the same officer and locals if I thought their identity might be revealed. "Officer" refers to both Sonoma Police Officers and Sheriff's deputies. I have also changed some street names in reports. If any of the fictitious names I've made up happen to be that of someone living in Sonoma, that is merely coincidental and not intentional by any means.

I read 30 years of Police and Sheriff's reports from the Sonoma Index-Tribune for this book. While there are some odd and funny crimes, the vast majority of police work and reports revolves around serious incidents that have detrimental effects to people and society. I want to thank the Sonoma Sheriffs and Police for their commitment and bravery in protecting both the town and county of Sonoma.

20% of the profits of this book will go to Arts Programs for low-income kids and other charities in Sonoma.

20700920R00136